TUTORING FOR PAY

ABOUT THE AUTHOR

Doctor Carpenter has taught and served as an administrator in both urban and suburban public school systems in New York and New Jersey since 1947. She retired in 1984 after spending ten years as a Superintendent of Schools. Now she devotes her full time to writing. She earned her Ph.D. at New York University in 1973 and graduated with a Founder's Day Award. She has been listed for many years in Who's Who of American Women.

TUTORING FOR PAY
Earn While You Help Others Learn

By

BETTY O. CARPENTER, Ph.D.

CHARLES C THOMAS • PUBLISHER
Springfield • Illinois • U.S.A.

Published and Distributed Throughout the World by

CHARLES C THOMAS • PUBLISHER
2600 South First Street
Springfield, Illinois 62794-9265

© *1991 by* CHARLES C THOMAS • PUBLISHER
ISBN 0-398-05714-1
Library of Congress Catalog Card Number: 90-46377

With THOMAS BOOKS *careful attention is given to all details of manufacturing
and design. It is the Publisher's desire to present books that are satisfactory as to their
physical qualities and artistic possibilities and appropriate for their particular use.*
THOMAS BOOKS *will be true to those laws of quality that assure a good name
and good will.*

Printed in the United States of America
SC-R-3

Library of Congress Cataloging-in-Publication Data

Carpenter, Betty O.
   Tutoring for pay : earn while you help others learn / by Betty O.
Carpenter.
     p. cm.
   Includes bibliographical references and index.
   ISBN 0-398-05714-1
   1. Tutors and tutoring. I. Title.
LC41.C28 1990
371.3′94—dc20   90-46377
                                     CIP

ACKNOWLEDGMENTS

Thanks go to Ms. Rosemary Krider Schmid for her assistance and excellent advice. She is a teaching professor at the Central Piedmont Community College in Charlotte, North Carolina whose specialty is teaching American English to foreign speakers.

CONTENTS

TUTORING FOR PAY

Chapter 1

INTRODUCTION

If you are like the rest of us, you must have, at one time or another, thought about starting your own business. And while you were thinking, you must have wished that there could be something you could do to earn money without having to go out to work every day—something you could do without being someone else's employee—something you might even be able to do from your home. And on top of that, haven't you wished that there might be a business of some sort that you could go into without an investing a lot of money? And wouldn't it be wonderful if it was something that could take advantage of the skills you already have and the things you already know? There is.

One of the best business opportunities available today to people who want to work for themselves rather than for someone else, who do not have much money to invest in starting up a business, who would like to work on their own terms and on their own schedules, who want to take advantage of their own skills and their own experiences and share them with other people, is tutoring for pay.

Advantages Of Tutoring

Tutoring has many advantages, especially if you are hoping to have a flexible work schedule, one that will not tie you down to regular working hours or the regular workweek of a salaried employee.

Among the advantages are the following:

- Tutors can set their own hours.
- They can set their own fees.
- They can work with as many clients, or as few clients, as they wish.
- They can work full time or part time, all year or only during certain months of the year.
- They can work with children, with adults, or with both.
- They can, to a very significant extent, do things their own way and

try innovative methods whenever they think there is a chance that they might be successful.

- They can work in rooms in their own homes or in other facilities away from home.
- They can work without the direct supervision of a boss or they can choose to work as an employee under supervision.
- They can concentrate on providing help with school subjects or they can choose to tutor in any of a myriad of other areas having nothing at all to do with academics. (Some of these areas will be suggested in later chapters of this book.)

One of the most attractive aspects of tutoring is that tutors are always working with other people in interactive situations. Thus, they never need to feel isolated and they always have the opportunity to learn from others as they are tutoring. In addition, tutors have the satisfaction of helping their clients to achieve something which is important to them, something those clients may not have been able to master before and surely would not have been able to master by themselves without assistance.

Ask any teacher about what the best part of teaching is and you will almost always hear that it is the satisfaction of watching the learning process occur, seeing the light in the eyes of the student who has grasped something new and now understands what may always before have been a muddle. That satisfaction—watching others learn and being responsible for bringing that learning to them—can be yours and you can earn money in the bargain should you decide to become a paid tutor.

What Does A Tutor Do?

A tutor helps people learn. That sounds simple enough, but it is not a simple process. And what is more, it is not "teaching" in the classic sense of teaching. Tutors concentrate on what their clients are *learning* rather than on what they are teaching.

Many people, adults and children, go through daily life feeling less than adequate about something they would like to do but can't, something they would like to know but don't. If only there were someone they could go to for help, they think, perhaps they could learn to do it, learn to understand it. But are there such helpers available? Of course there are. There are people all around them from whom they can seek help, but too frequently such folks are hard to find and not too willing to devote their time to becoming helpers.

Should you decide to become a tutor, you will be one of those specialists who is available to those who want to learn something. You will have made the decision that this is the way you want to spend your time. And once you have made that decision, you will want to get the message out to the public that you are ready and able to help people learn.

The way you will do that—to begin with—will be by advertising and spreading the word in the community. Soon people will notice your advertisements, hear others talking about your tutoring service, or perhaps pick up a brochure or flyer which you have distributed. The material which you prepare will lead folks to think that perhaps they can find and profit from the one-on-one or small group assistance you are offering. If your advertising is successful, they will seek instruction from you, and if your tutoring is successful, your clients will, at last, begin to deal with those areas in which they have always wanted to develop abilities but either have not been shown the way or have not understood adequately when they were shown. It will be exposure to repeated advertising by you which will stimulate the hope in such folks that tutoring will help them do what they have never been able to do before. And if your advertising finally does catch their attention, they will soon be calling on you for help.

And when they do call, what is it that you, as a tutor, will do?

Tutors provide a learning environment, instruction and learning assistance for people who are seeking to improve their knowledge or skill in specific areas. This assistance can be in academic areas like reading, mathematics, science, social studies or other school-related subjects. Or the assistance can be in non-academic areas like art, music, dance, drama, speech, bridge, chess, golf, computer, cooking, child care, sculpture, ceramics, woodworking, auto mechanics, or almost anything else that requires skill.

Most people would be able to tutor someone in something.

Parents and other adults, for instance, have always tutored children in all kinds of skills as the children grow and develop, even though they do it casually rather than for pay. They help babies learn to speak; they help in the process of socializing growing children by conveying to them what is and is not acceptable behavior; these are essentially tutoring processes.

In primitive societies, almost all of the children's education comes from the adults who surrounded them. There are no such things as schools as we know them. The children learn what they need to know by watching and doing, trying and failing, trying and succeeding, and then practicing.

In more advanced societies, we relegate large chunks of responsibility for the education of the young to schools. The schools succeed with most of the students but fail with a great many. It is from the ranks of those for whom the schools have not been a success that the tutor's clients will come if remediation is what the tutor is offering. (Of course, remediation is not the tutor's only choice.)

Tutoring for pay is not, can not be casual. It requires planning and preparation. The major purpose of this book is to help those who wish to tutor for pay to prepare themselves, to make solid plans, and then to succeed as tutors.

Why Is Tutoring In Demand?

When we speak of tutoring, one of the first things we think about is the task of helping people learn to read. Many adults can't read well enough to order from a menu, to understand what is written on signs, to get any information from a daily newspaper or from a set of written directions or even to read a story to a child. Many are unable to read a book or a magazine to fill out a form in a doctor's office or even to fill out an application for a job. People who are handicapped in this way are considered to be "functionally illiterate."

There have been nationwide advertising campaigns aimed at the functionally illiterate, trying to encourage them to recognize their difficulty and admit to themselves that they are profoundly handicapped by their inability to read. It is hoped that once having made that admission, they will be wise enough to seek help. Some few have been convinced and have sought help in various volunteer programs that are now available, but there are many who feel embarrassed to take assistance in public situations. They don't want to be seen at centers where this kind of instruction is offered for fear that people they know will see them and they will be labled as non-readers. There are also some who feel that if they are going to be tutored they want to pay for it. And there are also folks whose free hours do not match those of the offering institution.

It is obvious, then, that many people will seek help from private tutors once they know such tutors are available to them. And if you are going to be a tutor, one of your main jobs, especially early on, is going to be to get that message across. But helping non-readers learn to read, although both interesting and challenging, is by no means what tutoring is all about. That kind of activity is only one small corner of a surprisingly vast, available market.

In addition to people who are reading-handicapped, there are also a considerable number of adults who cannot deal with basic arithmetic. They have grave difficulty when trying to manage their finances, follow a recipe, or even to figure out whether they are being charged correctly at a supermarket. Some of them cannot even tell if they are being given the right change. They just hand over bills to cashiers and hope for the best.

In this complex world of credit cards, taxes, checking accounts, assessments, bank statements, bills and the dozens of additional monetary demands which are made on individuals every day, many people become confused. They would welcome, and they would greatly benefit from, help in understanding the practical arithmetic that is so much a part of all of our daily lives.

Some adults want instruction in leisure-time activities like bridge, chess, golf, tennis; some others seek practical instruction in such things as cooking, auto mechanics, flower arranging, electronics, and carpentry. Some will enroll in classes at local community schools—when those classes are offered. However, classes in the particular subjects people look for are not always available and community schools are not always easily accessible. A tutor can provide instruction in practical skills like these in a local home or a meeting hall. Instruction can be offered to individuals or to small groups.

Tutoring for children is always in demand. There are some students in every school class who are unable to keep up as the class progresses. For one reason or another, they sit in their classrooms and fail to learn what is being presented. Some are slow to grasp what is being taught and need much more repetition than what is provided. Some have missed one or more crucial lessons because they were absent from class when those lessons were offered. Some are unable to concentrate in a classroom environment. And some who learn slowly just become discouraged because others seem to be able to learn much more quickly than they can. Whatever the reason, once students fall behind, failure seems to build on failure. And those who fail begin to dislike school, teaching, learning, and experiences having anything to do with formal instruction. It takes a great deal of effort to overcome this kind of negativism.

Sometimes schools provide tutoring assistance for failing students during the school day. This usually involves pulling them out of class to get that help. These "pullout" programs often exacerbate the students' problems because they cause them to miss even more classwork while they are trying to catch up with what they had missed before. And often they feel so negative about the school environment that they resist learning anything from anyone while in a school.

In spite of that, schools continue to try. Sometimes they use teachers on staff to provide periodic individual tutoring to students who need it during the school day or after school. At other times the school hires non-staff people to provide that tutoring. Such non-staff employees are generally hired on an hourly basis and are assigned to a specific roster of children.

Schools which hire instructors for in-school tutoring provide special opportunities for tutors. By applying for these positions, tutors are able to take a step into the local educational system without losing their status as independent contractors.

When students fall behind, parents are usually alerted by the school staff. Whether or not in-school tutoring is available, many parents seek help for their children from private tutors. It is their hope that a tutor, who will work individually with their child in concentrated sessions, will succeed where the classroom teacher has failed. If the tutor is skillful, this parental decision is a good one and pays dividends. The child begins to succeed. It is evident that students will very often learn more, more easily, and more quickly in a tutoring situation, if for no other reason than the one-to-one concentration a tutor is able to provide on the unique problems the student brings to learning.

Some parents are not looking for remediation but rather for enrichment for their children through tutoring. They look for special classes in such things as creative writing, arts and crafts, acting, astronomy, woodworking, a specific foreign language, needlework, athletic clinics, swimming, etc. After all, music lessons and dancing lessons, which children have been taking for years, are really the most classic of all tutoring sessions, sometimes provided on a one-to-one basis, sometimes on a small group basis. Specialized tutoring in such areas as speech, to correct speaking defects like lisps, difficult intonations, or even foreign accents, is often sought after.

These days many parents seek pre-school classes for their youngsters (an hour or two a day, two or three days a week is what they look for) so their children can learn to play with other children in a safe environment.

A tutor who can instruct hearing people in the use of the signing language of the deaf can be fairly certain of attracting clients.

A tutoring area that has recently become popular (and always seems to be in demand) is "dog obedience" training. Tutors who plan to do this work are well advised to take training themselves in working with animals before offering any instruction.

Opportunities to tutor are abundant in most communities, not only in cities and large towns, but also in rural areas. It's up to the potential tutor, you, to identify the existing opportunities and then to prepare yourself to take advantage of them.

What Can You Expect To Learn From This Book?

Since there are a multitude of opportunities for you out in the marketplace if you want to tutor for pay, the important thing is to be able to identify each of those opportunities and then make them work for you. This book will help you to do that.

In addition, the book offers the following:

- Many specific content suggestions for tutoring success in particular academic and non-academic subject areas;
- A variety of practical tutoring approaches;
- Sound business advice;
- Advice for setting up and maintaining an office;
- References to additional information sources.

With all of this information and advice at hand, this book should serve as a handy guide and companion for you as you begin to tutor for pay. In addition, whether you have had a college education, a few years of college, or even if you never went to college (or indeed if you have never finished high school), there may be special talents and skills you have which you can share with others. This book will help you to do just that in a variety of ways:

- You will be shown an easy way to identify your own skills so you know exactly what you can offer to a student.
- You will find help in setting up your tutoring service as a business. This help will include suggestions on how to get started, how to keep student records and business records, how to keep track of your earnings and expenditures, where to find materials and where to find clients and tutoring opportunities.
- You will learn how to discover what regulations exist in your state, county and city that you may have to meet when conducting a tutoring service.
- You will find practical assistance in identifying the markets that exist in your community for the services you wish to offer.
- You will learn how to design advertising presentations that will bring clients to you.
- You will learn how to schedule your time so that it is used most profitably.
- You will learn how to expand your business so that you (eventually) might have other tutors working for you in your own learning center.

Using This Book

You will probably find that the most helpful way to use this book will be to read through the whole of it to get the flavor of what it is trying to tell you. That way, you will pick up suggestions in areas you may not have considered as applicable to you. After that, you will find it easy (by using the table of contents) to return to those specific sections which you feel can be of most value to you at any particular time. As your business takes off and begins to grow, you will find additional sections helpful. The book should continue to serve as a handy reference, both in the beginning—as you launch your service—and in the future as it expands.

The table of contents lists each chapter and the subheadings within each chapter. This organization will help you find the specific sections to which you wish to refer for information or suggestions. The Appendices at the back of the book contain illustrative charts, graphs, and other material referred to in the text. In addition, you will find a Glossary which provides definitions of terms used in the text, explanations of the ways in which those terms are used, and illustrative sentences to further clarify meaning. There is also a separate Bibliography, even though most of the books referred to in any of the chapters are fully cited as part of the text.

Every attempt has been made to make the textual content clear, easily readable and easily understandable. We hope you will enjoy using the book and will enjoy as well, from the outset, success as a self-employed person who is tutoring for pay and earning while you help others learn.

Chapter 2

GETTING STARTED

Whenever we begin something new, start a project, launch an enterprise we have not been a part of before, there are various preliminary steps to take which help prepare us for the tasks ahead. We are going to suggest a course of action for you to take as preliminary steps to launching a tutoring business.

Even though you may want to jump right in and reach out for clients immediately, if you are truly serious about starting a tutoring business and hope to become a successful earner through tutoring, we advise slow and steady progress at this beginning stage. There are several steps we feel it would be wise for you to take right from the start. The first set of these ought to be centered around yourself, around getting to know yourself in ways which you may not have taken the time to discover until now.

Since you want to tutor and you want to earn money doing it, it is important for you to be quite certain about exactly what field or fields of tutoring would interest you most. An easy and very effective way of finding the answer for yourself is to conduct a thorough self-assessment.

But why should you bother to do that? Isn't such an exercise nothing more nor less than a waste of time? After all, don't you already know yourself well enough without having to go to the trouble of conducting a step-by-step evaluation of who you are, what your talents are, and just what it is you are able to do well enough to share the skill with others? Perhaps. But in the next several months, if you are determined to become a paid tutor, you are going to be called upon to describe your qualifications and talents to a variety of potential clients, sometimes at the spur of a moment, often in public or on the phone. That can be a difficult thing to do. It is not easy to tell people about yourself if you do not have a long time in which to do it. Too often, you may inadvertently leave out some rather crucial pieces of information, information which may have made the difference in whether or not you were hired by a specific client.

The self-assessment effort we suggest you make at this early stage in your planning will prepare you to respond to questions about yourself fully, with ease, without stumbling or hesitation, with the confidence that potential clients have a right to expect from someone whom they will be paying to help them learn.

Are You Qualified To Be A Tutor?

Almost everyone knows something that someone else might want to learn. That is true of you, too, whether or not you have had any formal training to do the things you do well. Many of those special skills you have you did not learn in schools or classes (your hobbies, for example). Of course, some of your special skills you might well have learned in school. But no matter where you learned what you know, if you know it well enough you may be able to help others learn it.

In order to tutor some things (high-school subjects for example), you will need to have had a formal education—probably a college education. For tutoring many other things, you may not even need a high-school diploma. The lady down the street makes the most beautiful hand-stitched patchwork quilts and she learned how to make them from her grandmother who never got beyond the eighth grade in school.

Tutoring is not merely a matter of helping people to learn reading, writing, arithmetic and academic subjects. It is also helping in just about every field of work or play that occupies people's time and interest. If you know how to do something that others may want to learn to do, a tutoring opportunity exists.

Take a minute, now, to think about yourself and your unique talents and skills.

- Are you an athlete? A sports expert?
- Are you a superior cook with marvelous, unique recipes?
- Do you bake wonderfully?
- Do you make memorable house parties?
- Were you an English or a math major?
- Were you laid off because your plant closed even though you were an expert at what you did? Can you teach others that skill?
- Are you an excellent organizer?
- Are you a fast and accurate typist?
- Do you know how to use a computer?

- Are you an experienced word processor?
- Do you paint? Make sculpture? Do crafts?
- Are you good at games?
- Do you love to read? What are your favorite kinds of books?
- Would you be willing to conduct book discussion sessions?
- Do you write (books, stories, poems)?
- Do you enjoy helping children to learn?
- Do you have a lot of patience?
- Do you enjoy helping adults to learn?
- Do you dance, sing, play a musical instrument?
- Are you good with your hands? (carpentry, plumbing, house repair, auto repair, furniture)
- Do you speak, read and write more than one language?
- Could you teach English to foreigners?
- Are you able to teach speech, aerobics, drama, swimming?
- Do you know the signing language of the hearing impaired?
- Are you a lifelong smoker who has given up cigarettes? Can you help others give them up?
- Do you know a great deal about dieting, nutrition, health?
- Do you have special training in the techniques of parenting?
- Are you skilled in training animals?
- Do you enjoy spending time with pre-school-aged children?
- Can you make a patchwork quilt?
- Do you knit, crochet, cross-stitch?
- Are you an excellent marksman?

There are people everywhere who would like to learn more in every one of these areas and in other areas as well. For example, there are two women in the middle west who are in the business of teaching other busy women how to organize their houses and apartments so that their living quarters require a minimum amount of effort to keep neat and clean.

All kinds of people seek all kinds of instruction. This becomes evident when we casually thumb through most popular magazines and find page after page of advertisements offering self-help tapes, do-it-yourself manuals, and learn-at-home instruction. It is evident as well when we see all the adults who are trying to return to high schools to earn diplomas they rejected when they were younger, hoping that this time they will be able to sustain an interest in school subjects. And it is also evident when we realize how many people take coaching courses in preparation for special standardized examinations like GRE's (Graduate Record Examinations) and SAT's.

What is missing from the self-help, learn-at-home, back to high school, general coaching course offerings is the personal interaction, the back-and-forth attention a tutor, working singly with a client, can provide. What is missing is the specific answer to the specific question that the student is puzzling over, and the specific personalized guidance available at precisely the moment when it is needed. Only a private tutor can provide that kind of assistance. You can provide it. You can personalize instruction, provide answers to questions and help people learn. And you can be paid for doing it. This book is written specifically to help you learn how to do it.

Take another minute. Go beyond your skills and talents and think about your own special wants and needs as a working person.

- Do you want a flexible work schedule?
- Do you want to supplement the family income?
- Are you able to start with a small amount of extra money and build your business gradually, or must you earn significant money in income right at the outset?
- Are you homebound because of yourself or others in the family? Are you mobile and able to work outside of your home? Do you want to work close to home?
- Are you retired but anxious to do some kind of work, especially work with people? Would some extra money come in handy?
- Do you want to work for an organization like a community school or a trade school?
- Have you some special skills you can offer to a corporation? Do you know that some corporations sponsor yoga classes during work breaks? Some offer aerobic classes. Some provide infant supervision for employees. Do any of these areas appeal to you?
- Do you want to work with or without supervision? Does that matter to you?
- Can you set up small "at-home" classes?
- Have you access to a potential "classroom" which will enable you to work outside of your home should you wish to do so?

These are some, but by no means all, of the questions you ought to answer for yourself as you weigh your options with reference to becoming a paid tutor. Reexamine all of these questions. Answer them for

yourself. List the questions and your answers and keep these lists handy.
You will be referring to them in working up a self-assessment.

Self-assessment

Once you have begun to think about yourself, your skills and your
talents, you are ready to take another important step, which is to develop
a formal, written, self-assessment. The easiest and most productive way
to begin is to focus on the things you know about yourself.

- What specific things do you do every day?
- What do you do only once in a while that is special?
- How do you enjoy spending your time?
- What kinds of jobs have you held?
- What do you consider to be some of your major successes?
- What training have you had that you have never actually used for
  the purpose of earning money?
- What work have you done for pay?
- What work have you done as a volunteer?
- What are the things you do that your family, friends and co-workers
  always compliment you on?
- What special gifts (talents) do you have?
- What are the things you do that you just do not like doing?
- What do you wish you could do but have always been afraid to try?

Now look at the following SELF–ASSESSMENT CHART I. Reexamine and think about the answers you jotted down next to the questions
you asked yourself in the exercise above. Those answers should help you
evaluate your skills. They should also help you to decide what it is you
know, what it is you can do and what you can help others learn. Be sure
to add more lines if you need them.

SELF–ASSESSMENT CHART I

THINGS I KNOW I DO VERY WELL
(List everything that comes to mind   _____
including active hobbies like crafts,   _____
passive hobbies like reading, your   _____
talents and skills, and particular areas   _____
of learning at which you now excel   _____
or have in the past excelled.)   _____
                                             _____

THINGS OTHERS TELL ME I DO WELL
(List anything other than what you
have already put down in first
section.)

_____

_____

_____

_____

_____

THINGS I ENJOY DOING
(List what you like to do whether or
not you feel you do them well—like
reading to children, playing games,
helping older people, gardening,
cooking, etc.)

_____

_____

_____

_____

_____

_____

_____

THINGS I DISLIKE DOING
(List things you most dislike doing.)

_____

_____

_____

_____

Now examine your answers in the first two sections of the chart. Rank each of the items you have entered.

- Place a 1 next to those things you most enjoy doing.
- Place a 2 next to those you enjoy somewhat.
- Place a 3 next to what you find tolerable.
- Place a 4 next to what you hate to do.

You will probably have more than one item bearing the same ranking number. Rate each the way you really feel, not the way you think you ought to feel.

All of us participate in activities which we know we do well and which others have told us we do well but which we do not like to do. It is important at this stage that you recognize the areas you would rather not work in and avoid them if you can. Since you are going to be starting your own business, you have the option of constructing it in such a way that you will love doing what you will be getting paid to do. There is no better way to spend your working life.

You are now ready to place the items you have just ranked into the first column in the following SELF-ASSESSMENT CHART II. List them with your 1's first—and then in descending order. Now go to the column headed FORMAL TRAINING. Indicate where you learned each of the listed skills. Under whose training in what kind of formal setting did you develop the talent you have. (For example: SCULPTURE—ART CLASSES IN COLLEGE; READING INSTRUCTION—TEACHER METHODS COURSES IN COLLEGE.) If you had no actual formal training, indicate the circumstances under which you acquired the ability listed. (For example: GARDENING—OWN GARDENS; BRIDGE— SOCIAL PLAY, DUPLICATE TOURNAMENTS; MEDITATION— YEAR OF CLASSES WITH TRAINER; SIGNING LANGUAGE— INTERACTION WITH HEARING–IMPAIRED FRIENDS AND FAMILY.)

If there is anything on your list of talents and skills that you have recognized as something you particularly dislike doing, cross out the line. (For example, you may sew very well but dislike doing it. Cross out sewing.)

When you have completed the exercise, you will have developed a portrait of yourself as a potential tutor. You will be able to see just what you have to offer to others, even some things which it hadn't occurred to you that you might be able to tutor before you went through this exercise. You will see as well exactly what your qualifications are for tutoring in those areas.

Remember, whether your training has been formal or informal, you have acquired the skill. You are now ready to help others acquire it.

SELF–ASSESSMENT CHART II

TALENTS AND SKILLS	FORMAL TRAINING	INFORMAL TRAINING
————————	————————	————————
————————	————————	————————
————————	————————	————————
————————	————————	————————
————————	————————	————————
————————	————————	————————
————————	————————	————————
————————	————————	————————
————————	————————	————————
————————	————————	————————
————————	————————	————————
————————	————————	————————
————————	————————	————————

(Make as many copies of the charts in this book as you think may be useful to you.)

Your Needs

Now that you have identified your talents and your skills, the next step is to evaluate what your special needs are. Since you do have needs, taking a good look at them in this planning stage will help you to keep from making the kind of decisions you may later regret, such as trying to do too much too soon. Again, a chart will help clarify things for you.

On the following SPECIAL NEEDS CHART, some individual needs are already listed. These are examples. You have thought about your needs while going through the exercise you did at the start of this chapter. Go back to those pages now and refer to them as you fill in the spaces on the chart. Extra lines are available for you to give you the opportunity to add to the suggested list. You will undoubtedly have needs or wants which are very personal and very specific to you. Add even more lines if you need them. Cross out any of the needs listed that do not apply to you and substitute others that do. Remember that you are doing this for yourself and you want to get as accurate a picture as possible.

Under the column marked PRIORITY, next to each of your needs indicate whether you think the item rates **TOP** priority consideration or **LESS** than top priority. Under the column headed FLEXIBILITY, indicate the degree of flexibility you have with regard to each of the items. Use the words **VERY, SOME, NONE.**

Even though you may have indicated that something needs priority consideration in your planning, you still might feel you can be somewhat flexible about it when it comes to the point at which you are considering specific offers. For example, if a steady income is a top priority for you but you feel you may, under some circumstances, be somewhat flexible about it (like being offered a large fee for periodic work), you will be able to see at a glance that you have options on what action to take under what special circumstances.

Under the column headed OTHER, add comments as ideas occur to you which might help you in the future as your plan to become a paid tutor takes shape. Things that ought to be noted in this column are any certifications, degrees, or licenses you may hold, or any prizes or special recognitions you may have earned which may make you more attractive to clients as you offer assistance in particular areas.

SPECIAL NEEDS CHART

NEEDS	PRIORITY	FLEXIBILITY	OTHER
Steady Income			
Health Insurance			
Flexible Hours			
Work Nights Only			
Work Days Only			
Work Mornings Only			
Work Afternoons Only			
No Supervision			
Independence			
Work In Home			
Work Away From Home			
Work With Children			
Work With Adults			

Now you are ready to examine all of the charts you have made. It will help if you post them on a wall where you can refer to them all at the same time. ("Post-it" tape is excellent for this purpose because it holds paper and yet leaves no marks on your walls when you take the paper down.) Your examination should show you several interesting things that you may or may not have known about yourself before you completed these exercises. You should be able to see at a glance:

- What you are able to offer to a client.
- What you are willing to offer.
- What you are unwilling to do.
- What kind of time you have available.
- How flexible you are willing to be about time or tutoring areas.
- Whether you will be seeking to help adults or children, or both.
- Whether you will be working from your home or from somewhere away from home, or both.
- Whether you will be seeking to work for a school, a corporate organization, strictly for yourself, or for a combination of clients.
- What your top priorities are.
- What your areas of flexibility are.

You have now completed some of the important background work in preparing yourself to launch your new business and you are ready to take some additional, very practical preparatory steps.

Chapter 3

CONSIDERATIONS IN
LAUNCHING YOUR BUSINESS

If you choose to work at something which will provide you with an income, large or small, and you are not on the regular payroll of another party, you can be said to be in business. This is true whether the income you are receiving is regular or periodic, large or small, the result of part-time or full-time work.

And if you are in business, you will learn very quickly that even though we live in a free-enterprise society, all businesses, large and small, are regulated by local, state, and federal requirements. From the one-man show to the largest corporations, all must conform to these requirements. Thus, when you decide that you are going into business, even one as seemingly private as a tutoring business, you are going to have to learn what these official requirements are and learn what you must do to conform to them.

Regulations can differ from state to state and sometimes even from city to city. Because this is so, we cannot provide you with a list of specifics which will apply to you. It will be up to you to find out what is expected of a small business in your particular location and in your state.

Since you will be tutoring for pay and since you will probably not be an employee on the regular payroll of a school or of any other organization, even if you decide at some point to do per-hour or per-day consulting work for them, you will undoubtedly fall into the category of the "self-employed." You are certain to find that there will be rules and regulations specific to earners who are self-employed and it will be to your benefit to learn what these regulations are in the beginning when you are first starting your business.

Dealing with formalities may seem like a formidable undertaking to you right now, but you will find that it really is not as bad as it appears to be. Getting the information you need will not be difficult and, as a bonus, you are certain to learn a great deal about how your local government works.

Some Important Things To Learn About

Listed below are a variety of suggestions concerning matters which you may have to deal with:

1. Many communities expect everyone running a business of any type to acquire a business license or permit. Your community may be one which has such a requirement.
   - The fees for such permits are usually small and the applications are generally not hard to fill out.
   - The place to inquire about licenses or permits is at your town or city hall or at your county seat.
   - Do not be reluctant to ask for help in completing and filing any applications or other papers if you feel you need such assistance.
2. If you plan to give your business a name other than your own (for example, THE A-1 LEARNING CENTER), you will probably have to take some steps to make that business name legally yours.
   - Taking these steps will keep anyone else from using the name you have selected.
   - In addition, it will keep you from making the mistake of using someone else's name.
   - Again, the fee for this name protection will generally be just a few dollars.
   - Once more, you can inquire about what to do to obtain this protection at your local town or city hall.
3. If you plan to tutor at home and to use a room in your home as your business office as well as your tutoring site, it will be important for you to check the zoning regulations in your community.
   - Zoning is usually the province of a county, but there may be local city or town zoning ordinances controlling what may and may not be done in a home in certain residential neighborhoods.
   - Small businesses, like tutoring conducted in the home, as long as they stay small and only provide private lessons to one person at a time, are generally not in conflict with the zoning laws.
   - However, it would be prudent, so that you may avoid having to

pay any fines in the future, to check the rules which apply in your community before making decisions about where to set up your service.

- If you find that your home is in an absolutely restricted area and no business of any sort at all may be conducted from it, before you give up hope take the time to find out how you can apply for a zoning variance. Such a variance might allow you special consideration. It may or may not be granted, but at least you can try.
- If a variance is not granted, you still have a number of options concerning where to tutor. These will be discussed at some length in an upcoming chapter.

4. Another vital consideration for you to attend to at this time is a social security number.
   - If you have one, there is nothing more you need to do about it.
   - If you do not yet have your own personal social security number, it is essential that you apply for one immediately since all working people in America are expected to have them.
   - You will have to contact the Social Security Administration office in your area and register for a number.
   - You will find the location of the office listed in your local telephone directory.

5. You may have to modify the insurance you carry on your house if you are going to use your home as a base for the tutoring you do.
   - You will need to check the status of the insurance you carry to determine what it covers and what it does not cover.
   - Your local insurance agent is the person who will have the information you need and the one who should be very helpful in advising you.

6. If you are planning to work with children, your state may have some special licensing requirements which you must meet.
   - Requirements such as these may or may not not apply to tutors who provide instruction on a per-session basis.
   - You should check these regulations by calling your State Department of Education, office of licenses and certifications.
   - Describe what it is that you are planning to tutor and the client group from which you expect your students to come.
   - Ask for specific advice concerning what you may and may not

do with the credentials you now hold, as well as how to obtain the additional credentials they may advise you that you need.

- You may also have to meet a set of conditions concerning your tutoring site depending on the age of the children you plan to work with and the number of children you plan to gather together at any one time.

These suggestions for action on your part may sound complicated and like a lot to have to do, but in reality everything that needs to be done can be done quickly and easily. Keep in mind that conforming to local regulations is for your protection and the protection of your business, as well as for the protection of your future clients. A little bit of foresight at this stage can keep you from having to backtrack later.

Preparing To Talk To Officials

As you can see, you are going to have to be in contact with people in a variety of governmental offices in order to get the answers you need to questions concerning the start-up of your business, as well as to be certain that you are doing everything that ought to be done. There is some advice we have to offer which we believe will serve you in good stead whenever you need to seek answers from official sources.

Since a visit to a government office can be a rather confusing experience, because of the intricacy of the special bureaucracy that exists, and since it is almost inevitable that you will be dealing with more than one person in more than one office, it is easy to be sidetracked and fail to get the precise information you came for. A little pre-visit or pre-phone-call planning can be quite helpful. Try doing the following:

1. Write each question you wish to have answered on a three-by-five index card and don't leave the office you are visiting, or put down your phone receiver if you are calling, until you are satisfied that you have gotten a precise, reasonably understandable answer to each of your questions.
2. Jot down on the card the name and phone number (and extension) of the person who gave you the answer, the date you received the response and the main points of the advice given to you.
   - This is not only good for record keeping but will help you later when you want to remember or to refer to exactly what it was that you were told.

- You will also know who to call if you need further clarification, who is likely to be helpful, and who to avoid speaking to if you need to contact that office again in the future.

3. Be sure to have a number of "What if . . . " questions on your cards. These will help clear up for you what the consequences might be if you fail (willingly or only accidentally) to follow the advice you are being given.

   - Often you will find, interestingly enough, that there are no important consequences should you choose not to follow that given advice.
   - Sometimes this kind of "What if . . . " question will provide you with important information you hadn't even thought to ask about.

4. Be sure that one of the cards you prepare bears the question, "IS THERE ANYTHING ELSE I OUGHT TO KNOW ABOUT . . . (licensing, permits, certification, self-employment regulations, insurance, fees, etc)?" Too often you only get answers to the questions you actually ask and you may not be aware that there are others you ought to ask.

A single visit to your county office and one to your town or city hall should provide you with all the business information you need concerning licenses, permits, regulations and rules, especially if you have written down all of your questions beforehand. Make notes as you get your answers. Do not be embarrassed to do this. Good notes will be really helpful to you once you are back in your office trying to recall exactly what it was that you were told.

As indicated above, one call to the State Department of Education's office of licenses and certification should give you the answers to questions about whether you need to obtain any credentials, exactly what credentials you should have, and what you must do to go about obtaining them.

The Small Business Administration

The United States government supports a bureau which has as its primary purpose providing help to individuals who are trying to establish themselves in small businesses. It is aptly called the Small Business Administration (SBA). Its main offices are in Washington, D.C., but there are local offices in large and small cities throughout the country. The location of these local offices can be found by consulting your local telephone directory. They are listed under "United States Government— Small Business Administration."

Since the Small Business Administration has a variety of pamphlets available, free of charge, which offer specific advice to help you in planning and setting up a business and since it also has consultant time available, it might be well for you to pay a visit to their office and ask to meet with one of their consultants. In addition, the Small Business Administration might be able to assist you in obtaining a start-up loan if you are willing to adhere to the demands of its specific requirements. Generally, the SBA itself does not actually lend you money, but it will assist you in obtaining a loan from a bank or elsewhere. Their experts may also assist you in filling out their forms. You lose nothing but a bit of time by paying them a visit and you may gain a great deal.

One of the questions you might wish to discuss with the people you consult with at the SBA offices (as well as with your own accountant) is the advisability of incorporating your business. There are are pros and cons attached to incorporation and these differ somewhat from state to state. Once more, it will be helpful to you to learn as much as you can about what these may be before deciding on what action, if any, to take.

Remember that the Small Business Administration may be able to guide you at various times, even long after your business is up and going. Keep their numbers handy and the names of their consultants in your files.

Setting Up Your Office

Once the formal considerations are out of the way, it is time to concentrate on setting up your office. This may or may not be the same place in which you will do your tutoring, but it is the place where you will keep all of your clients' records, your files, your financial records and other information pertaining to your tutoring business.

If you are going to work out of your home, you ought to devote a whole room to your tutoring and not use it for anything else. If you do, that room can then become a tax asset for you, since you will be able to deduct its cost from your income tax. If it is not possible for you to set aside a full room as an office, it would be wise, at least, to cordon off a section of one of your rooms, perhaps even screen it off, and keep that section only for your business use.

Eventually, you may be earning enough to rent an office away from home, but unless you have substantial start-up capital, it might be unwise to obligate yourself to meeting a monthly rent payment when you first launch your tutoring business.

In order to set up an office you will probably have to make a small investment in furniture and equipment. To begin with, you will need all or most of the following things:

- A desk or a table devoted to your work
- A lamp and a comfortable chair
- A telephone and, if possible, an answering machine
- A file cabinet and file folders
- A bookcase or shelves on which you can keep your reference materials and books you will use with students
- Stationery with your name or your business name on it
- Business cards
- Pens, pencils, a sharpener, paper clips, a stapler, sharp scissors, paste, and a good typewriter, or, if you can afford one, a personal computer and a printer
- Scrap paper and white-out
- Access to a copying machine
- A good flexible date book with enough space for you to enter appointment times and places and to jot down appropriate helpful notes
- A briefcase
- Anything else you are used to having at hand when you do paperwork.

Right from the very beginning you should make it an unvarying practice to keep receipts and other documentation for everything you spend for your business, no matter how small the amount. Expenditures add up and they become very important when the time comes for you to consider your tax liability at the end of the fiscal year.

Along with all other expenditures, keep a record of your car mileage when you are driving anywhere related to your tutoring business. In addition, keep records of what you spend on tolls, telephone calls, meals, parking, books, reference materials, in fact any and all of the expenses related to your tutoring. Keeping accurate records is an essential part of running any business. (An entire section of this book will be devoted to simplified, easily "doable" record-keeping practices.)

You should try to set up your office so that it is as comfortable and attractive a place to work in as you can make it. You will be spending a great deal of time there and so will your clients. Because of this, it would be wise to have places to store your papers, your supplies and equipment, and anything else which might otherwise be scattered about. A few pleasant pictures on the walls might be an asset. Good lighting is a necessity. A student work space with a straight-backed chair and a table or small desk at which he or she can work must be available wherever you plan to hold your sessions with students. It might also be helpful for you to have an easle, a pad of newsprint, and a set of magic markers. These are an adequate substitute for a chalkboard in most situations and they are easily portable.

A Quick Overview and Checklist

You have taken the important first steps to prepare yourself to become a paid tutor—a self-employed person in charge of your own business.

- You have contacted the appropriate governmental offices to learn what is expected of you when you are starting up a business enterprise.
- You have obtained the necessary permits, credentials, insurance, and even zoning variances.
- You have spoken to the consultants at the Small Business Administration offices and have taken advantage of their expertise.
- You have an office which is equipped with the hardware (machines and furniture) and software you need to function as a business.
- You have decided on where you are going to do the major part of your tutoring.
- You have set up your tutoring site so that your students can feel comfortable and be in pleasant surroundings while they are learning.
- You know just what it is that you want to tutor, what clientele you plan to target, and what qualifications you have that will help you convince potential clients that you can help them.
- You have determined whether or not you will need start-up funds to launch your business and where and how to get them if you do.

• You have decided whether or not you wish to become a corporation.

The obvious next step is going to be the search for clients. You are prepared. Now you have to connect with those people out there who need your help.

Chapter 4

PREPARING TO FIND CLIENTS

S ome of the approaches you will use in seeking clients will differ to a degree, depending on whether you are looking to the tutoring of children, or adults, or both. Because of this, now would be a good time to reexamine your self-assessment papers so that you can clarify those choices for yourself.

If you plan to work primarily with children, the methods you will use for contacting and finding clients will center primarily on the schools and on school-based activities. They will differ as well, depending on whether you are looking for students who are not succeeding with their schoolwork and so need remediation, or whether you are seeking students who want enrichment activities of one sort or another. If you plan to work primarily with adults, you will have to tailor your messages even more precisely, depending on just what it is you plan to offer.

Where and what you advertise will have to differ, for example, if you are offering reading instruction for the functionally illiterate from what it would be if you are offering activities like crafts courses, dancing, or auto mechanics. But even though you will be specializing when you actually begin to tutor, perhaps in one area, perhaps in several, there are some general first steps you will want to take in attracting clients of any sort. In this chapter we will cover both the general and the specific.

First Steps To Take In Seeking Clients

Success in getting students to choose you as a tutor will depend on how well you are able to communicate—to get your message out to the public so that they will know about your service. What you will need to start with, even before you do any formal advertising, is a set of documents that you can present to interested potential clients. These ought to provide them with an attractive picture of you. They should tell who you are, what your skills are, what you can do to help those who hire you, something about your availability, and enough practical material to make it easy for potential clients to contact you. In other words, you need to prepare a portfolio of materials which you can use to introduce yourself to potential clients. These should be so attractive that they make it easy for you to sell your services.

Your Portfolio

The carrying case, or "portfolio" itself, need only be a file folder or a notebook, or a report cover with pockets which can hold your material. But you may wish to buy a more substantial, more elegant case. You will be carrying it with you to various meetings, so think about what kind of case will suit you and enhance your image.

The contents of your portfolio should always be at hand wherever you go on business, especially when you are going to be where you may find potential clients. They should consist of papers you want such clients to see and perhaps keep, as well as other things which you might find useful in firming up contacts.

1. Always carry at least a dozen copies of a one-page resume consisting of accurate, easy-to-read material providing information about you and your special qualifications for the job you hope to do with the people you will tutor.
   - The resume should stress the particular aspects of your background which highlight the information and the kinds of skills you are prepared to share with students.
   - You may want to have more than one resume, each of them stressing different skills, especially if you are going to be tutoring in more than one field. (NOTE: Advice on how to prepare an appropriate resume can be found later in this chapter.)
2. Always carry a number of your business cards and leave them with folks, hand them out, post them if possible, or otherwise distribute them whenever you have the opportunity. (NOTE: Suggestions for designing a business card can be found later in this chapter.)
3. You ought also to keep at hand three or four copies of each endorsement and/or letter of reference which you may have obtained from instructors, supervisors, or other persons who can attest to your competence in the areas you wish to tutor.
   - If you have no such letters, it would be advisable to contact several people you have worked with professionally or as a

volunteer and ask that they write letters of recommendation for you. These can be important in helping a potential client to feel confidence in your ability.

- Do not carry the originals of these letters. Make copies. It would be hard to replace originals and you may sometimes want to leave a copy with a potential client.

4. Carry copies (not originals) of any certifications, permits, and/or licenses you may have which are pertinent to the tutoring you are planning to do. You may be asked whether you have such credentials and it makes a good impression to show them rather than only to claim that you have them.

5. Always keep your date book with you. You may find that you have to make appointments on the spot and you should know when you are going to be free and when you will be busy.

6. Keep two or three of your business checks with you. You may need to purchase something, or provide a donation to an organization, or make some other kind of unanticipated expenditure. It is always better to do that by check than in cash, since checks provide you with a paper trail for easier record keeping.

Developing Your Resume

If you are seeking to work with individual clients, why is it necessary for you to have a resume at all? Can't you just tell people about yourself when you meet them? Shouldn't that be enough? It might be, if everyone had a good enough memory. However, most people don't.

A resume paints a portrait of you. It does it quickly and does it in a limited space. What's more, it can be left with potential clients and thus serve as a ready reminder to them of who you are, what you do and how to find you. It also establishes you as an organized person, someone serious enough about the tutoring you provide to have made an investment in yourself.

On the next several pages you will find four examples of resumes which can be used as models to assist you in preparing those you may wish to use. These models are suggestive. You may choose to use some other format. As you begin to work on your resume, you ought to go back and consult your self-assessment charts. They will be particularly helpful to you in deciding what to include and what to leave out.

There are some basics which should appear in every resume. You will

find them repeated in each of the examples presented as models. They
include, of course:

- Your name, address, and telephone number (and the name of your
  business if that is different from your own name).
- The major topic headings under which you will spell out your
  unique qualifications and the experience you have had which is
  pertinent to the tutoring you are planning to do.
- The particular service(s) you are offering and the credentials you
  have for offering it (them).
- At least one reference.

You may feel that a single resume with all of your qualifications
included will be enough to serve for all the work you plan to do. On the
other hand, you may wish to prepare several different documents, each
stressing different aspects of your talents and skills.

We have found that it is helpful to the potential client if the specific
skills they are seeking in us are stressed on our "vita" sheet (resume).
Including too much can sometimes overwhelm a reader. On the other
hand, including too little can fail to present you as a person with a rich
enough background to be able to do the job.

The four resumes that follow are different from those you might wish
to use if you were seeking a tutoring position as an *employee* in a school
or a corporation. In presenting yourself for that kind of job, the format
of your resume would allow you to be more inclusive; you would want to
put greater emphasis on your academic background and formal training.
A model for that kind of resume, along with additional helpful hints,
will be found in Appendix A.

The four model resumes in this chapter are designed to provide just
the very specific information about you which clients are likely to want
when they are seeking to learn something from you. They are purposely
slanted and kept sparse so that they can stress a particular set of your
capabilities, the ones most pertinent to the service you are offering.

For practical reasons, your resume should not be longer than a single
page. Remember, you are going to want to give them to people. Con-
dense your material so that one page will be all that you need. If you are
typing it, use a good bond paper. If you are going to have it printed, use a
good quality stock. Stick to white, off-white, pale beige or pale gray and
very dark ink. Design your paper so that there is a great deal of space
without print (wide margins on all four sides). That will make it easier to

read and more attractive to the reader. Remember that your goal as a tutor is to find and keep clients. This means you want to be just specific enough to be impressive without being overwhelming.

Your resume is your letter of introduction. You want it to reflect you and to make the best possible, most lasting impression. The important thing about these models is that they are all about the very same person but stress different things.

Sample Resume No. 1

Cynthia D. Harrow
4321 Pinegrove Drive
Charlotte, N.C. 28226
(704) 268-9876

SKILLS	*Can provide learning assistance to students who are having little success in mastering the basics including reading, math, spelling, usage, and handwriting as well as other subjects taught in elementary school.*
EXPERIENCE	*Worked successfully as a volunteer tutor for three years in the XYZ program of the YMCA.*
	Provided individual help in the classrooms of Crossroads School while working as a teaching assistant for five years.
	Substitute teacher in elementary grades in four of the county schools.
	Served as a tutor in the Future Teacher's program at Central High School during senior year.
CREDENTIALS	*Associate Degree in Elementary Education.* *Substitute Teacher Certificate*
OUTSTANDING ATTRIBUTES	*Patience* *Understanding of children* *Ability to motivate children to want to learn*
REFERENCES	*Personal—Ms. Genevieve Danielle* *3412 Eastway Court* *Charlotte, N.C. 28226* *(704) 282-4683*
	Professional—Dr. C.B. Jones—Principal *County School # 6* *Mooresville, N.C. 28115* *(704) 663-6633*

Fees and schedules will be discussed at initial conference.

Sample Resume No. 2

Cynthia D. Harrow
4321 Pinegrove Drive
Charlotte, N.C. 28226
(704) 268-9876

SKILLS

Can provide learning assistance to students at any academic level. Can teach English to those who are foreign speaking. Have strong interest and capability in liberal arts and math even though primary training was in science.

TRAINING

Science major with Master's Degree in Biology. Minor in Chemistry.

EXPERIENCE

Research Biologist for Dyn Inc. (7 years)

Professor of Bio-Chemistry at P.C.U. (25 years) Successful volunteer tutor in local high school. (6 months)

Substitute teacher on day-to-day basis in high school science classes.

CREDENTIALS

Substitute Teacher Certificate

OUTSTANDING ATTRIBUTES

Strong educational background
Many years of teaching experience
Knowledge of how to help students learn

PRESENT STATUS

Retired

REFERENCES

Personal—Ms. Genevieve Danielle
3412 Eastway Court
Charlotte, N.C. 28226
(704) 282-4683

Professional—Dr. C.B. Jones—Dean
Science Department, P.C.U.
Columbus, N.J. 08180
(609) 446-4466

Fees and schedules will be discussed at initial conference.

Sample Resume No. 3

Cynthia D. Harrow
4321 Pinegrove Drive
Charlotte, N.C. 28226
(704) 268-9876

SKILLS	*Party Bridge and Duplicate—All Conventions*
	Backgammon
	Chess
	Scrabble
	Gin Rummy
	Mah Jong
EXPERIENCE	*Played all above games for years with private groups and in tournaments*
	Taught many beginners the rudiments of the games, privately and in groups, and arranged for practice and competition
	Conducted classes in the RST Community School for 3 years
CREDENTIALS	*Hold ten masters points for Bridge.*
	Compete with high scores in computer Scrabble.
	Win frequently on top level against computer Chess and computer Backgammon.
OUTSTANDING ATTRIBUTES	*Patience*
	Enjoyment of competition
	Ability to assist beginners, intermediate players and experienced players who wish to improve.
REFERENCES	*Personal—Ms. Genevieve Danielle*
	3412 Eastway Court
	Charlotte, N.C. 28226
	(704) 282-4683
	Professional—Dr. C.B. Jones—Principal
	County Community School
	Mooresville, N.C. 28115
	(704) 663-6633

Fees and schedules will be discussed at initial conference.

Sample Resume No. 4

Cynthia D. Harrow
4321 Pinegrove Drive
Charlotte, N.C. 28226
(704) 268-9876

SKILLS	*Expert at providing instruction to adults:*
	Reading
	Handwriting
	Arithmetic
	Speaking
	English as a Second Language
EXPERIENCE	*Worked successfully as a volunteer tutor for three years in the XYZ program of the YMCA.*
	Provided individual help in the classrooms of Crossroads Community School for five years.
	Taught several members of my own family to read and write.
CREDENTIALS	*Life experience in these areas*
	Read and write English fluently
OUTSTANDING	*Patience*
ATTRIBUTES	*Understanding the needs and desires of adults who are handicapped by not knowing how to read, write, and/or do arithmetic.*
REFERENCES	*Personal—Ms. Genevieve Danielle*
	3412 Eastway Court
	Charlotte, N.C. 28226
	(704) 282-4683
	Professional—Dr. C.B. Jones—Director
	YMCA Adult Education Program
	Mooresville, N.C. 28115
	(704) 664-9876

Fees and schedules will be discussed at initial conference.

Remember when you develop your resume that you need not be, nor claim to be the world's greatest expert in an area in order to help someone learn. What you need is some competence, some knowledge, some patience and a strong desire to provide assistance. These are the things you have to sell. These are the things your resume should stress.

Designing A Business Card

A local printer will always be ready to help you design or select an already designed business card which will be appropriate for your needs. They have books full of samples to help you decide on what you want, so by all means consult with one or more of them.

Do not order more than 500 cards to start with. (You probably will not be able to order fewer than 500 since most printers won't print fewer than that number.) The reason you do not want too many cards to begin with is that after a while you may want to change the address of your office, your phone number, or even the design of the card. Give yourself the option to be flexible.

When you go to the printer (for both cards and stationery) bring along some of these ideas.

- Keep your card both simple and elegant. In the tutoring business you will do better if you can inspire confidence from the first contact you have with a client.
- Be sure that the printing on your business card is raised. Raised printing makes a better impression. The same holds true for your stationery.
- Don't use colored stock unless it is a very pale gray or beige. If you can, stay with white and use either dark blue, black or very dark brown ink for lettering. Those inks stand out better, are generally easier to read, and make a better impression on a prospective client.
- For the same reason, easy readability, don't use fancy printing.
- If you use a logo, keep it small and be sure it is appropriate for what you want to tutor.
- Be sure the name of your service (if you have one), as well as your own name, address and phone number, are prominent.
- On either bottom corner or all across the bottom of the card, indicate exactly what services you are offering.
- Most business cards are printed across the width of the card. Some

people, for the sake of being different, print the card so that it must be held lengthwise to be read. This is not a good idea for a tutor. Stay as simple as possible and as easy to read as possible.

Your business card could look something like this:

CYNTHIA D. HARROW   *(704) 282-4683*
4321 Pinegrove Drive, Charlotte, N.C. 28226

TUTORING

Individuals and Small Groups
Increase Understanding — Improve Performance
Learn New Skills

Special instruction in: Reading, Math, Handwriting,
Speaking and all Academic subject areas.

Use your imagination. Design your card so that it pleases you and so that you will be proud to hand it to people.

Grammar, Spelling And Punctuation

A word of caution is in order here. In all of your preparations it is essential that you present yourself as someone who is knowledgeable. Nothing will spoil your image as a tutor as quickly as a misspelled word or bad grammatical constructions. Check and recheck everything you write and everything you use to get the attention of the public.

Because it is so very important for you to be correct, it is essential that you obtain an up-to-date dictionary and that you *USE* it. There are many different dictionaries available, but one that is particularly easy to use is *Merriam Webster* soft-covered pocket dictionary. It is small in size, easy to keep on a desk near you when you are writing, easy to carry around in a briefcase, and it is an excellent reference book. It is available in most local bookstores and will probably fill the majority of your dictionary reference needs. A copy of a good thesaurus will also prove to be very helpful.

Two additional books which you may find useful are *Sisson's Word and Expression Locater*, and *The Synonym Finder* by J.I. Rodale.

Many colleges, universities and libraries throughout the country maintain reference lines and it is possible to call them for help with a grammar or usage problem. Consult your local telephone book, or directory assistance, for the reference office in the institution nearest you. One handy home reference for grammar and punctuation (there are many available) is *Warriners English Grammar and Composition* published by Harcourt, Brace, Jovanovich and available in most bookstores. Another is *Understanding and Using English Grammar* by Betty Azar.

Complete citations for all of these materials will be found in the Bibliography section at the back of this book.

Chapter 5

OTHER BUSINESS PREPARATIONS

Y ou now have a portfolio which contains your resume, your business cards, your date book, letters of recommendation and credentials and whatever additional material you feel may be useful to you to help you introduce yourself to potential clients. You know that you are qualified. You know exactly what kind of training you have had which makes you qualified, and you are ready to do the kind of tutoring work you would like to do.

We may, at this point, be accused of letting a warm idea freeze to death, but there are just a few things you still ought to do before you actually begin to actively advertise for clients to work with. One of the most important of these to put into place is a bank account.

Opening a Bank Account

Since your tutoring activity is going to be a business—even though it will be one in which you will probably be self-employed—it will be to your benefit to open a bank account either in the name of your business, if you have such a name, or in your own name. You will certainly want to have such an account if you have incorporated.

For sound business reasons, this bank account should be kept separate— apart from any personal account you may have, even though you may (or may not) wish to use the same bank. You ought not to have any trouble opening a separate business account, but the bank may require that you keep a minimum balance in it. For both accounting and record-keeping purposes, it is always best to keep all of your business matters, not just your bank accounts, from becoming mixed with those of your household.

The bank account you open ought to be a checking account which is interest producing. You may have to shop for such an account since not all banks offer them to businesses as readily as they do to individuals. This kind of account will give you maximum flexibility in making deposits and withdrawals, in paying for purchases, and in settling your bills, and it will produce some interest income for you at the same time. Your checkbook will also help you to maintain records of your expenditures. If you get into the habit of paying for everything that you buy for your business with checks, the cancelled checks themselves will serve as receipts, as well as a running record of what you have spent. If you keep your balances properly, you will always know the current state of your finances.

It also may be to your advantage to establish, early on, a relationship with a bank in the name of your business since there could come a time when you may wish to float a loan (for purposes of expansion, perhaps). Having been a bank customer for a period of time will stand you in good stead in such circumstances.

Be sure to take the time to examine and review your bank statements each month to be sure all of your checks have cleared and to be sure that your earned interest, if any, has been correctly posted. Follow-up on any discrepancy either with the bank, or in the case of uncashed checks, with the vendor holding the check.

If your students pay you with checks, be sure to deposit them as quickly as possible so that you do not foul their records either. Cashing checks promptly is considerate and is, at the same time, a good business practice.

We have mentioned several times that keeping accurate records is a vital part of running a business. You will find that you are going to need to keep at least two kinds of records:

- Business Records—consisting of indications of income and expenditures.
- Student Records—consisting of student activity and achievement.

Business Records

If you make it a policy to keep accurate business records from the outset, you will have little difficulty in documenting your finances as your business grows. Be assured that there comes an occasion when almost every business is called upon to produce actual documentation of income and outgo.

It is easy to set up a record-keeping system that does not take much time or attention and yet will provide you with readily accessible, reliable information any time you need to have it. Buy a large, manila, "accordion folder" and a package of self-stick file folder labels. Type or clearly print your labels as follows:

- 100—INCOME
- 200—OVERHEAD
- 300—OFFICE EQUIPMENT AND SUPPLIES
- 400—EDUCATIONAL SUPPLIES AND MATERIALS
- 500—BOOKS, MAGAZINES AND TAPES
- 600—OTHER EXPENSES
- 700—MEMBERSHIPS
- 800—CHART OF ACCOUNTS
- 900—FINANCIAL STATEMENTS

Attach one of these labels to the top of each of the expanded file sections of the accordion folder so that they can be seen easily. For record-keeping purposes the pockets in the accordion file are now ready to be used to hold your memos, receipts, and notes for the year.

There is one thing to remember before you put anything into this file. BE SURE TO DATE EVERY PAPER AND EVERY OTHER ITEM BEFORE YOU FILE IT.

At the conclusion of each fiscal year, you will be able to tie up this accordion folder and store it away with all of its memos, receipts, bills and other papers securely filed in it. That way you will always have it for reference purposes in the future. And it will be easy to start a new folder for every new year.

Within each major numerical category, you will be able to identify several subcategories. Exactly what these subcategories may be will, of course, be up to you, but some suggested subcategories are given here.

Remember, before you insert anything into the accordion folder, enter the date and the appropriate Chart of Accounts number on it. Do this for each paper or other item you file. This will make your bookkeeping, when you get to it, very simple.

The following suggestions should also be helpful to you as you set up your business records:

1. Once you have determined what your overhead costs are (rent, electricity, heat, telephone, etc.), be sure to file individual slips for those expenses each month and don't forget to date the slips. There are rule-of-thumb ways to figure your overhead costs:
   - If your office is in your home and you live in a seven-room house and you keep one of those rooms set aside entirely for

business, one-seventh of your rent, or of your mortgage payment, one-seventh of your electric bill, one-seventh of your basic telephone bill plus charges for all of your actual business calls, and one-seventh of your heating bill may be charged to your business as actual overhead expenses.

- You should consult with your accountant before making any final determinations on exactly how to figure your overhead expenses.

2. Get receipts for everything you spend including receipts from the post office. Mark each receipt with the Chart of Accounts number appropriate to it and date it before filing it.
   - The Chart of Accounts recommended below may not contain enough subcategory numbers to adequately describe your operation. If you need additional numbers or you find that there are some you don't use, alter the numbers to suit your own needs. The numbers are not what is important. The system is. Make it work for you.
   - You may find it useful to insert ordinary manila file folders into the accordion pockets and to label these with the subcategory numbers (101, 102, 103, etc.). Such subdivisions will make it even easier for you to file information and much easier to access it when you need it.
   - You may want to paste a copy of the INDEX FOR THE CHART OF ACCOUNTS on the outside of your accordion folder and keep another copy in your 800 file. Both of these will serve you as handy, quick-reference sheets when you want to find a particular paper.
   - So that you can use them in this way, you ought to make several copies of the INDEX FOR THE CHART OF ACCOUNTS which follows.

Spread Sheet

In Appendix B, you will find a spread sheet which will help you to see your business year at a glance. You might wish to take a look at it now. Listed down the left side are the numbered categories from the INDEX FOR THE CHART OF ACCOUNTS. Across the top are the months of the year. In the boxes where they intersect, there is room for you to enter DOLLAR amounts pertaining to each category.

Index for Chart of Accounts

---

100 — INCOME
    101 — Income from individuals
    102 — Income from schools
    103 — Income from organizations
    104 — Interest income
    105 — Other income

200 — OVERHEAD
    201 — Rent
    202 — Electricity
    203 — Heat
    204 — Telephone
    205 — Other

300 — OFFICE EQUIPMENT
    & SUPPLIES
    301 — Furniture and hardware
        (Typewriter, Stapler, etc.)
    302 — Files and record keeping
        supplies
    303 — Software, typewriter
        ribbons, paper, pencils, tape
    304 — Postage, envelopes, shipping
    305 — Copying and printing
    306 — Other

400 — EDUCATIONAL SUPPLIES
    AND EQUIPMENT

    401 — Student Materials
    402 — Student supplies
    403 — Audio and visual tapes
        and recorders
    404 — Other student needs

600 — OTHER EXPENSES
    601 — Mileage
    602 — Conferences & Workshops
    603 — Meals
    604 — Miscellaneous

700 — MEMBERSHIPS
    701 — For Students
    702 — Professional
    703 — Community
    704 — Other

800 — CHART OF ACCOUNTS
    801 — Copies of Index
    802 — Spread Sheets
    803 — Other

900 — FINANCIAL STATEMENTS
    901 — Bank Statements
    902 — Cancelled checks
    903 — Tax Documents
    904 — Other

The entire 100 category is devoted to income, and your entries with regard to income should be made in a color other than the one you will use for entries on expenditures which will be made in categories 200 through 700. Using different colors will help keep you from becoming confused when it comes time to total up the SPREAD SHEET at the end of your fiscal year.

As your business grows you may wish to create an entirely separate spread sheet for the 100 category, since it is referring only to income, even assigning separate 100 numbers to each of your clients. This can be done by giving each client a separate number and also a letter which reflects his last name. Thus, if 101 refers to client income as it does in our suggested chart, 101.1D may be income from Davis, 101.2D may be income from Duke, 101.3R may be income from Reynolds. (The letter would be there primarily as a convenience for quickly finding a client's account.) You may wish to use a similar breakdown in each of the other 100 categories.

Both at the end of the 100 section and after the 200 through 700 section, you will find lines for totals.

At the foot of the page there is a line for netting your monthly operation. This is done by subtracting the total of your expenses (the total of categories 200 through 700) from your income (the total of all one-hundreds).

If you have a net loss rather than a profit, you will have to subtract your total income from your total expenses and label it with a minus or place brackets around the amount to indicate that it was a loss.

Your net profit or loss for the entire year will be totaled into the box on the far-right, bottom corner of the spread sheet. Adding each line across and each line down should result in showing you how your business has fared.

Categories 800 and 900 and their subcategories are for filing papers and official documents related to processes and to record keeping, and so they do not appear on the spread sheet.

Because it enables you to see your business year at a glance, this spread sheet ought to be a great help to you in making business decisions and in filling out tax forms and other business statements throughout the year.

The spread sheet in Appendix B has been condensed so that it would fit on one page. To be useful, we suggest that you enlarge it so that it covers the width of at least two pages. This way, you will have enough room to make all needed entries on the appropriate lines in the appropriate months. If you are constructing your chart from ordinary eight-and-a-half by eleven paper (graph paper might be helpful), attaching two papers along their edges, matching edge to edge and taping their backs will give you a natural fold and a sturdy hold.

Student Records

When you are tutoring individuals, whether they are adults or children, they like to feel that they are important to you and that you remember, at least as well as they do, what has happened in each of the sessions they have shared with you. They are especially keen on your remembering what went on in the most recent sessions. Because this is true, it is essential that you develop the habit of keeping accurate records of your sessions with each client so that you have material to refer to which will refresh your memory about what occurred. If you have only a few clients, remembering may not be much of a problem, but if you have many, you will almost certainly confuse one session with another.

That is the reason it is a good idea for you to have a file drawer in which you can keep student records. A paper file carton can serve you in the beginning if the cost of a filing cabinet is more than you wish to spend before you begin to earn some money, but eventually a filing cabinet ought to be purchased.

The folders you use for student records may be letter-sized or legal-sized (because they hold more) but should definitely be the pocket-type files. These look flat when you buy them, but they expand. They have closed sides and are much like envelopes so you can drop notes into them without fear that they will fall out of the sides. They can be labeled on their closed sides and on the top tab-section.

If you jot a brief summary of what has happened in each session as soon as your client leaves, and date the note, you will have a running record of all you have done with every student during every one of your tutoring sessions. Records such as these are a treasure trove if and when you consult with parents or review progress with the student. They will be particularly valuable when you are working with adult clients because you will be able to recall incidents they may have forgotten. No matter how good a person's memory is, it is not good enough to remember many small happenings over long periods of time. Your records will, without a doubt, serve both you and your students much more accurately than either your memory or theirs could possibly do.

Student record folders ought also to contain all of the test and evaluation data pertinent to their progress, as well as important samples of their output from the time you begin to work together right up through the time they are going to leave you. Those samples should serve as an almost self-explanatory history of what the student has learned and how he or she has grown. They can also serve as documentation for your success should you need such references in the future.

From time to time, you and your student might wish to tape something to go into the record. Encourage your students to do this. Playbacks at future sessions are often dramatic motivators, inspiring them to greater efforts. It is a good idea to not only permit students to review their records when they request such a review but actually to schedule time for such an inspection periodically. Go over all of their work and be sure to indicate where, how much, and in what ways they have progressed. Such reviews ought to bear little resemblance to school report cards, especially if you are working with students needing remediation, but even with others.

You, as a tutor, ought never be concerned with grading a performance. You should work with students until they have grasped what they need to know and can function knowledgeably in the area. If they cannot, there is no point in rating them with a "D." What your task is in such instances is to find other ways to help them learn. Remember, especially when you are doing remedial work with a client, that bolstering an ego almost never hurts anyone. In fact, positive reinforcement based on truth generally helps everyone to perform better.

Chapter 6

FINDING CLIENTS

This is the point at which *who* and *what* you wish to tutor become really important considerations. You will need to design one set of approaches for finding clients who are children and another set for finding clients who are adults.

In both instances, however, it would be a good idea for you to do the following:

- Make a great many contacts. Get out to as many functions in the community in which you plan to work as you can. Join some organizations. Make it your business to be where it is likely that you will meet new people.
- Let people know about the tutoring service you are offering and present yourself and what you do with enthusiasm.
- Advertise both formally, with hard copy and local media announcements, and informally by talking to people and encouraging them to talk to others.
- Introduce yourself to people who can help you meet clients.
- Be prepared to sell your service to prospective clients wherever and whenever you meet them.
- Do not be shy. People can only learn about you if you are ready and willing to tell them who you are and what you do.

Tutoring Children

If you have decided that what you want to do, at least to begin with, is tutor young children, the place to start looking for students is in the local schools. It therefore goes almost without saying that you should become familiar with those local schools. You will want to visit them and learn what you can about them.

The fastest way to obtain information is to call the office of the district superintendent and request a list of the district's schools and the names

51

and office telephone numbers of each of the school's principals. Offer to come by the superintendent's office to pick up the list or to pay the postage to have it mailed to you.

Once it has arrived, you will be able to call each principal and request an appointment to meet with her or him, and you will be able to personalize your request by using the principal's name. In all probability you will be asked by the school secretary why you want to see the principal. Tell the secretary as much of the following as seems appropriate:

- You are an interested member of the community.
- You are planning to start doing some private tutoring in the very near future.
- You are hoping to see the classrooms and the school building so that you may learn something about the educational environment of the students you will be working with.
- You would appreciate any time the principal might be able to spare for you.

Most principals will be happy to have you visit, and if they themselves are not able to spend some time with you, they will usually be able to arrange for someone else to escort you around the building.

Be polite and persistent in making your request. If it's not possible to agree on an appointment the first time you call, indicate that you will be calling again and then do call again.

Any time you can get to spend with a school principal will be invaluable to you, both because of what you will learn about the school environment and because of the impression you will leave on the principal. There may be a time in the future when he or she will remember you and recommend you to a client or even call you in to do some special tutoring work in the school.

Philosophy Of Learning

Prepare for those meetings with the principals. Be ready to talk about your approach to tutoring, the kinds of learning materials you use for specific instruction in each subject area and your educational philosophy. This ought to be (at a minimum) that:

EVERY CHILD IS ABLE TO LEARN IF HIS OR HER OWN POWER SOURCES ARE RELEASED AND GUIDED, AND

THAT INDIVIDUAL INSTRUCTION AND ATTENTION ARE
POTENT, POSITIVE KEYS TO RELEASING THAT POWER.

Be ready, as well, to talk about your fee structure if you are asked about it. You need not be specific about your rates, but you ought to indicate that you will be willing to discuss individual fees with individual clients based on the particular difficulty of the challenge the student presents and the particular circumstances of the family.

If you are pressed for an exact amount, you could indicate that your fee range is between twenty and thirty dollars a session for individual instruction and somewhat less for individuals if they are working in small groups. (There are tutors who earn between thirty and fifty dollars a session. You will have to do some exploring in your own community to learn what other tutors are charging and what the going rates happen to be.)

On your tour with the principal indicate that you would be willing (if you are willing) to tutor at the school on an hourly basis or a per-diem basis if your services can be used. Ask about what the hourly pay rates are for such instruction. That will be of some help in guiding you as you establish your fees for private work. Also ask about the kinds of credentials or certifications you might need were you to tutor in a public school.

Leave a copy of your special resume and your business card with the principal and willingly respond to any questions she or he may ask you about yourself. If you have developed a full professional resume (see Appendix A), you might want to leave a copy of that as well.

As you tour the building, take notes and ask questions. Be sure to jot down ideas which you might find useful in your own work. Try to spend some time in the school library (it might be called the learning center), even if you have to request permission to return at a later date. Browsing the shelves, speaking with the teacher in charge and examining available hardware and software will certainly give you ideas to use in tutoring.

Before you leave the school, ask the secretary to give you the date of the next PTA meeting. Attend at least one meeting in each school. Become acquainted with the concerns of the parents. Bring your business cards to such meetings. Hand them out to people you speak with. If there are materials available for distribution on a table, place some of your cards (or a flyer if you have one) on that table. Retrieve those that have not been taken by the end of the meeting so that you can use them elsewhere.

Attend at least one school board meeting. Bring your portfolio. In fact, you ought to bring your portfolio to any and all functions you attend in the community, including club affairs and religious gatherings. Let people know that you are seeking students to tutor.

Post one of your business cards on available community and church bulletin boards, in schools if possible, in gyms, and in supermarkets.

Write a thank-you letter to the principal of each school you have visited indicating your gratitude for the time she or he has spent with you. (A sample letter can be found in Appendix C.)

Use the telephone book and examine local newspapers to determine what tutoring services are currently available in your community. Call and speak with other tutors. Learn what they charge for their services. Find out if established tutoring centers need additional instructors. Offer to do some substituting work for them.

Call for appointments and visit the priests, ministers and rabbis of local houses of worship. Ask for a few moments of their time. Use those moments to tell them about yourself and the service you plan to provide. You may be asked to set up sessions in their buildings. Be prepared to accept or refuse, with reasonable reasons. Leave your resume and card and follow up every visit with a thank-you letter.

Prepare to advertise in local newspapers, penny-savers, church and organization papers. Your first ad can be a copy of your business card. Plan to advertise frequently. One-time ads are soon forgotten. Some people need to see an ad four or five times before they get around to responding to it. Additional ideas for creating advertisements can be found in Appendix D.

Be ready when that first call comes. It will probably be a call from a parent, since most children do not arrange for their own tutoring. Parents looking for a tutor for their child are going to want to know about you in that first conversation. Keep a copy of your Self-Assessment Charts and your resume in front of you when you speak to them on that initial contact. Those papers will help you to talk about yourself. Have a list of questions ready on a prepared INITIAL CONTACT SHEET—CHILD, to ask about the student and be sure to jot down the answers next to the question. What you may want to ask will be:

INITIAL CONTACT SHEET—CHILD

1. What is the name of the student?
2. How old is she/he?

3. What is the student's grade placement?
4. What are the tutoring needs the parents see as necessary for this child?
    - Remediation? What subject areas?
    - Enrichment? What kinds of activities?
5. How did the parent learn of your service? (The answers to this question might help you plan your advertising in the future.)
6. When can the parent and child meet with you for a first consultation?

Tutoring Sites

By this time you should have decided whether you are going to do your tutoring in your home, in the home of your clients, or in some other facility. Whatever your decision, that is the place where the first meeting should be held so that the student knows exactly where to come for regular tutoring sessions.

There are cautions to be observed with regard to each of the tutoring sites mentioned above.

1. If you tutor in your home or in another facility such as an office, you must rely on someone to bring the student to you unless he or she is old enough to come alone.
    - Parents and students both forget appointments from time to time.
    - From the outset be sure to make it clear that you will charge for any scheduled session not canceled in advance, since your time means income to you.
    - Provide both the parent and the student with a written copy of that statement.
    - Indicate that you, too, will make every effort to provide advanced warning should any necessary cancellation of a session occur.
2. If you tutor in your home, be sure that you do so in a room in which you will have privacy, one in which you will not be interrupted by other members of your household.
    - Your student is paying for and deserves to have your complete attention.
    - Turn on your telephone answering machine and do not respond to phone calls while you are working with a student. A client

can become very disconcerted if he or she has to wait while you
are on the telephone concentrating on someone else's problems.

- Make every effort to minimize all distractions so that you and
  your student can remain focused on the business of the session.

3. If you tutor in the student's home, do so only under the same
conditions:
   - A private room in which to work.
   - No family or friend interruptions.
   - No TV, no radio, no music.
   - No telephone.
   - No other distractions.

4. If you have access to an outside office which is safe and is conducive
for you to use as a tutoring site, by all means use it.

It is a good idea to offer a first session with each student as a free
consultation. That will be a time for you, the parent and the student to
meet and assess one another. It will give you the opportunity to determine the following:

- The extent of the problems you and the student will be dealing with
  whether the student is coming to you for remediation or for other
  tutoring (perhaps even advancement);
- The fee you will be charging for each session or group of sessions;
- The length of each of the tutoring sessions;
- A tentative schedule of sessions;
- A schedule for review, assessment and reporting sessions.

Your new client (and his or her parents) should leave this initial
consultation session with:

- A copy of your business card, your resume, and your policy for
  keeping appointments;
- Knowledge of your per-session fee, the length of sessions and the
  approximate spacing of regular evaluative consultation sessions;
- A schedule of tutoring sessions for at least the following month.

You should be sure to enter the schedule you have agreed on with the
client into your own date book. Do not delay doing this. Schedules
become confusing, especially if you have several clients.

You should have learned a great deal during this first meeting about
the child you will be working with, enough to begin to tutor at the start of
the next session.

Immediately after the student leaves, set up a client record folder. Insert the notes you took and sketch out your plan for beginning instruction at the next session.

Tutoring Adults

Making contact with potential adult clients will demand a somewhat different approach. One place to begin the search for clients may be the local community school. Whether or not you wish to tutor classes in the school, talking to the administrator of the school will give you some ideas about what people are looking for. It will also help establish the fact that you are looking for students who may need your help.

Make an appointment and go to the school for your talk. Get a feeling for what happens in a community school. Leave a copy of your resume and your business card with the school administrator. Be sure to write a thank-you note after you leave. (A sample of such a note that you can adapt for this purpose can be found in Appendix C.)

Call for appointments and visit the priests, ministers and rabbis of local houses of worship. Ask for a few moments of their time. Use those moments to tell them about yourself and the service you plan to provide. They may be very likely to know people in the community who would profit from working with you. Leave your resume and business card and follow up with a thank-you note.

You will have to advertise. Free advertising space exists on bulletin boards in churches, synagogues, stores and supermarkets, many of which will permit you to post one of your cards. If you do this, be sure to return and check periodically to be sure it is still there. Prospective clients sometimes will take the card rather than stand and copy the information they need.

Carry your cards with you and offer them to people at meetings of the clubs and community organizations you attend. Take every opportunity to speak at these meetings and explain what you do and offer your help to those who might need it.

Accept invitations to appear on local TV and radio talk shows. Hosts on these shows are always looking for interesting guests. Be prepared with some unusual information about your tutoring approaches and about yourself as well.

There are more formal ways to get your message to the people who may need tutoring. Some of these, like buying advertising space, can be expensive. Others can cost only a little. Some of the less expensive ways to broadcast your message are:

- Local penny-saver papers
- Local daily or weekly newspapers
- School newspapers and magazines which accept advertising
- Periodic newsletters of clubs, churches and synagogues
- Spot announcements on local radio and TV stations
- Flyers—Send some to personnel officers in local factories.

One of the most important things to remember about advertising, and we've said it before, is that repetition is vital. Don't rely on a one-time ad to get your message across. Sacrifice size if you have a limited budget, but keep the ad running. It will often take people several readings before they decide to contact you.

When you are contacted, offer the consultation meeting free. Be ready to tell your prospective client about yourself and to answer any questions she or he might have. Have your Self-Assessment Charts and your resume readily available for reference. They will help you to conduct those initial conversations with quiet control.

Almost all of the cautions and approaches discussed in the previous section on tutoring children also apply to tutoring adults. They are repeated here with slight modifications.

Have a list of questions ready to ask about the client on an INITIAL CONTACT SHEET—ADULT, and be sure to jot down the answers next to the prepared questions. What you may want to ask will be:

INITIAL CONTACT SHEET—ADULT

1. What is the exact spelling of your name?
2. What is your address and phone number?
3. What do you believe your learning needs are?
   - Remediation? What subject areas?
   - Enrichment? What kinds of activities?
   - Other?
4. How and where did you learn about my tutoring service?
5. When can we get together for a first consultation? (Be sure to indicate that there will be no charge for that session.)

By this time you should have decided whether you are going to do your tutoring in your home, in the home of your clients, or in some other facility. Whatever your decision might be, that is the place where the first meeting with your client should be held.

There are cautions to be observed with regard to each of the tutoring sites mentioned above when you are working with adults.

1. If you tutor in your home or in another facility such as an office, you must rely on the student to keep appointments.
   - From the outset, be sure to make it clear that you will charge for any scheduled session not canceled in advance since your income depends on filling your time profitably.
   - Provide the student with a written copy of that statement.
   - Indicate that you, too, will cancel in advance should it become necessary to change a scheduled session.
2. If you tutor in your home, be sure that you do so in a room in which you will have privacy and will not be interrupted by other members of your household. Your student is paying for and deserves to have your complete attention. Turn on your telephone answering machine and do not respond to phone calls while you are working.
3. If you tutor in the student's home, do so only under the same conditions—a private room, no family or friend interruptions, no TV, no radio, no music, no telephone.
4. DO NOT TUTOR IN THE CLIENT'S HOME IF YOU DO NOT FEEL COMPLETELY SAFE AND COMFORTABLE IN DOING SO.
5. If you have access to an outside office or classroom which is conducive to use as a tutoring site, by all means use it if you feel it is a safe place to meet.

Use the initial consultation as an opportunity to learn as much as you can about your client, but keep the session short—no more than half an hour.

Don't share confidences with him or her. Your's is to be a business relationship and it will serve you better if you maintain a degree of distance. It is fine to be friendly, but NOT TO BE FRIENDS. It is important to keep that difference in mind.

Your new client should leave the initial meeting with a copy of your business card, your resume, and your policy for keeping appointments. Clients should know your per-session fee and the length of each session. They should have a schedule of sessions for at least a month. Be sure to enter the schedule you have agreed on with the client into your own date book. You should have learned enough to begin to tutor at the start of the next session. Immediately after he or she leaves, set up a client record folder. Insert the notes you took and your plan for beginning instruction at the next session.

Tutoring Small Groups

The previous methods will serve in obtaining groups of clients, as well as individual clients, for such activities as crafts classes, bridge instruction, square dancing, cooking, sewing, etc. If you are registering individual clients but plan to group them with others for tutoring purposes, be sure to tell them so in advance. Generally, when groups are seeking an instructor they send one of their members to do their negotiating. Your initial meeting may be with an individual and you may have to offer a free trial session to the entire group before they agree to hire you. Be flexible and be prepared to demonstrate.

Chapter 7

GENERAL TUTORING METHODS

Whether you are tutoring children or tutoring adults, whether one-on-one or with small groups, there are certain basic understandings you ought to rely on. There are also some workable, and successful, tutoring approaches which you may want to use. These have to do not so much with the methods of instruction you choose to use in your tutoring as with the emphasis you place on what your students are learning. The most inspired instruction is worthless if the student who is the object of that instruction fails to learn.

Learning is aided by teaching, only aided. Learning is an active, not a passive process. In the process of learning, the student's active involvement is all important.

Understandings

If clients have come to you for remediation, it is a safe bet that classic teaching approaches have probably not worked for them. They have been to school. They have attended classes. They have used textbooks and done assignments. They have listened to "lessons." They have been "taught." Yet, they have, somehow, resisted learning. Perhaps, for a variety of reasons they may not have been able to learn. Students such as these would have little need to seek the services of a tutor if classroom instruction had worked for them—if they had learned what their teachers taught when that knowledge or skill was presented in their classrooms. But when students just sit in a classroom and let knowledge flow over them like water over a rock, it would take centuries to make any change in them. Merely attending classes and sitting through hours of teacher presentations hasn't been enough to make them learn. Even the use of varieties of attractive books and educational materials hasn't been enough to make them learn. If all the schools had to offer hasn't been enough, how can you hope to make a difference?

Knowing that these students have not learned much in their class-

61

rooms is exactly where your power to make a difference begins. Remember, these people had to attend school. Their attendance was required. But there is nothing that requires them to attend tutoring sessions. They are with you because they want to be. And they are paying to be with you. That is powerful motivation for learning. In addition, you know that ordinary classroom methods are going to be largely unsuccessful, even in a tutoring milieu. And you also know that how and what you teach is not what is crucial. The only thing that is going to matter for these students is what they are able to learn.

You will be most successful in helping your students learn if you try new and different approaches based upon setting up interesting, challenging learning situations in which they can be active participants. This approach will work not only for those needing remediation but for those coming to you for enrichment as well. Presented below are a variety of suggestions to help you do this kind of tutoring:

- Whenever possible, assist your students to ferret out needed knowledge and information for themselves. Give them assignments which rely on their doing this.
- Set up the classroom challenges, point the direction for finding answers and solving problems, provide source and resource material, and then be available to assist, especially with interpreting the importance of what the students have found.
- Discover and then make use of the unique learning styles of each of your students so that you may help each of them understand and retain what they have uncovered. (See "Student Self-Assessment" in a later section of this chapter.)
- Be sensitive as you observe how your students work on problems, and guide them within the scope of their abilities, helping them to stretch, but not pulling them beyond what they can manage without becoming frustrated.

As we have already indicated, when clients come to you for enrichment, it is equally important that your methods do not mimic those ordinarily used in the classroom. What you are tutoring will provide you with clues about how to tutor, but your approach, as with remediation, should always be to involve your student in doing, in seeking solutions and in finding new ways. The quickest way to lose students is to rely heavily on making information-filled presentations. Presentation-recitation lessons should be used very sparingly, if at all.

You should be able to help your students not only to uncover and discover but also to recognize they have discovered and to feel the excitement of learning. You should be able to help them gain access to data banks, to experts in the fields they are studying with you, to books, tapes, and other aides. For example:

- If you are providing instruction in instrumental music, an essential part of that instruction should be in helping the student learn the history and development of the instrument and to discover what particular music was written in what time periods for that instrument, as well as exposing them through records and tapes to the performances of renowned instrumentalists.
- If you are teaching something more esoteric, like astrophysics, you are going to want to help students seek and find what various experts believe to be essential questions and perhaps theoretical solutions to problems, not only to help them see what others see but also to think what no one has yet thought.
- If your students have come to you to learn English, especially English as a second language, you will certainly want to give them the opportunity to practice saying words, to listen to tapes, to read and hear simultaneously. They would be able to borrow such material, with your help, from local public libraries, especially from the children's section.

Remember, whenever possible, take your clues from your students on both how and what to offer and how long to remain with a particular activity. Then make your decisions. If clients come to you for group instruction, they, too, will expect you to be able to demonstrate, illustrate and then guide each group member toward individual success in the learning. Your approach, again, ought to be different from that of a classroom teacher. That approach depends on presentation, recitation and testing. Yours ought to be demonstration, encouraging individual performance, and assisting not only individuals but the group as a whole as well so that all can achieve competence. For example:

- If you are teaching square dancing, the square can only be successful if all four sets of partners are able to follow the calls well enough to do the steps. Special assistance may have to be provided to anyone who is slower to grasp the movements or who is lacking in coordination.
- Sometimes the best way to provide that extra aid is to help the

group develop a sense of responsibility for every individual in it. When a group begins to think of itself as a unit rather than as a collection of individuals, you will see much less competition, much more cooperation and generally better performance from all.

Even though when you are tutoring groups it may feel to you as though you are teaching a class, remember that your emphasis should never be on the teaching; it should always be on the learning and thus on the active participation of the students. Both you and your clients will achieve more, faster, and they will retain it far better if you always keep that fundamental truth in mind.

Before devoting time to discussing tutoring approaches specific to particular subject areas, it is important to explore some things tutors ought to do with all students, from the very young, up to and including the adult, from the fast to the slow learner. The rest of this chapter will be devoted to examining these kinds of universally applicable activities. Future chapters will be devoted to exploring methods which can be used in tutoring in specific areas.

Assessing Student Needs

One of the very first things you ought to think of doing when tutoring is to determine what your students know, what they can do, what they do not know and cannot do and what they hope to learn from you. There are both formal and informal approaches, as well as tests you can use, to make these determinations. Of course, which methods you use in evaluating what your students know will depend to a large extent on the subject matter you are going to be concentrating on, as well as the students' learning styles. To some extent it will also depend on your own preferences. Whatever method of evaluation you decide to use, since no student will come to you as a "tabula rasa" (a blank page), it will be necessary for you to find out what knowledge and skill he or she brings to the learning situation.

Most children have had their performance evaluated with a variety of standardized tests in school. You can generally obtain the results of these tests (the scores) from them and their parents. But if you'd rather get your own results, you can, of course, purchase standardized tests and administer them yourself. Adults will, in most instances, not have that kind of test results handy. They may never even have taken a formal achievement or diagnostic test.

Should you want to conduct a specific diagnosis with a test which has been standardized, you will be able to find and buy such instruments. To find out where they are available, call the education department, or the library of a local college or university, or the Office of Tests and Measurements of your State Department of Education, or even the office of your local Superintendent of Schools. Tell them what you wish to do and ask where you may purchase the kind of test you want to use.

The Educational Testing Service in Princeton, New Jersey can also be helpful; so can most libraries. Any college or university library should have at its reference desk a copy of the more than two thousand page volume which is called *Mental Measurements Yearbook*, originally written by Oscar K. Buros. The ninth edition was published by Gryphon Press in 1985 and was edited by James Mitchell. This book describes available tests and their uses and tells you where they may be obtained.

Although most of these commercially developed tests are of limited value in a one-on-one situation, some of them, especially those which are diagnostic, may help you construct your own evaluation devices. In addition, from time to time one or another of these tests may be useful if you find you need to provide a formal, standardized assessment result for one of your students so that you can report to parents or to a school.

One of the learning disabilities you will find some of your students have is an inability to take a standardized test without freezing. In such cases, practice on some of these instruments may be very helpful. There are techniques which can be learned which make test taking easier and which once learned will help calm anxiety. Some suggestions concerning taking tests can be found in Appendix E. For the most part, tests you make up yourself, both written and oral, will give you a substantially accurate and reliable picture of student performance and will probably be much less threatening to someone who has consistently done poorly on standardized tests in school situations. It goes without saying that tests you design yourself will be less costly.

Once you have determined the nature and extent of the difficulties your students are having, through formal or informal testing, you will be ready to take another step: helping the student to assess his or her present competence level and need for assistance.

Student Self-assessment

It is not only important for **you** to know where the student stands when you begin to work together, it is also important that your students know just what they can and cannot do. This will give them a benchmark to refer to, a starting point against which they will be able to measure their progress as they improve. You will find that even slow improvement will be encouraging to students if they are helped to see that they are actually learning.

A student self-assessment test should be administered by you, but not as a paper and pencil test. It ought to be an interactive exercise between you and your student. Your purpose is to help the students get to know themselves better. You should be the avid listener, the questioner, and the note taker. (Taking notes should be done as inobtrusively as possible.) In the course of the test, you should be able to pick up reactions which are beyond those you are directly asking for, and these student reactions should give you some additional insights into the learning problems the student has been living with.

The questions listed below are some you may wish to use in making up the test. They would apply either to children or adults seeking remediation and can be modified for use with people seeking other than remedial tutoring. There will certainly be other questions you believe to be appropriate. Feel free to add or substitute them.

For convenience sake, it will help you to use lined paper and to list all of the questions you will be asking on about one third of the paper at the left. This will leave you with enough space to jot the student's responses on the lines next to the questions. These papers should be prepared well in advance of the testing and you should show a copy of the questions to the student before beginning to ask them. It will go a long way toward removing any tension from the session.

You should ask the questions and jot the main points of the student's answers. Don't try for a verbatim notation and don't ask the student to repeat answers. That could cause students to feel self-conscious and could get in the way of subsequent answers. Use the student's name frequently when you are asking the questions. It will tend to put him or her at ease and will personalize the session.

You might decide to use a tape recorder for these assessment sessions, especially if you are uncomfortable taking notes. Should you use one, you will have a verbatim record of what was asked and answered and that could be quite useful in the future. If you plan to tape this or any other session in which students are involved, be sure to let them know that you are doing so and don't do it if there is any objection.

Example Of A Student Self-assessment Test: Remediation

- How well do you think you . . . (read, write, do arithmetic, spell, dance, sing, speak, etc. — depending on what they have come to you to learn.)
- Why do you think you do not do better?
- Do you think it is possible for you to learn to do better?
- How do you think I can help you to do better?
- How do you feel when you have to . . . (read, write, etc.)
- How would you like to feel?
- Do you think that is possible?
- What one (2, 3) ways do you like to spend time? Why?
- What do you dislike doing more than anything? Why?
- What do you think is important for me to know about you and how you learn?
- Why do you think working with me will help you?
- What is the first thing you want to learn in these tutoring sessions?
- What does your family think about this tutoring?
- Is there anything else you want to tell me?

Example Of A Student Self-assessment Test: Non-remediation

- Why have you come?
- What is it that you expect to learn from me?
- How much do you know already?
- Why do you wish to learn more?
- How do you think I can help you learn?
- What do you think is important for me to know about you and how you learn?
- How much time do you have to devote to practice besides what you do in these sessions with me?
- What is the first thing you want to learn?
- Is there anything else you want to tell me?
- Is there anything you do not particularly want to tell me but think I ought to know about you?

At the end of the session you should take the time to review the questions and all of the the answers with the student. Do not hesitate to make any corrections or additions he or she may wish to have made with reference to their test responses. It is their judgments on each of these matters that you are seeking and so it is important that they feel comfortable about the answers you are keeping as part of their records. Let them know that. It is not your assessment of them that this is about. It is their assessment of themselves. Date the paper (and the tape if you made one) and keep it in the student's folder.

From your tests of the student and your administration of the self-assessment test, you ought to have learned a great deal about your students and have come to some conclusions about what approaches may and may not work in your tutoring sessions. Specific suggestions designed to help you plan your sessions will be found under the subject matter headings in later chapters. In Appendix F, you will find a general lesson plan form which should be helpful to you in preparing for tutoring sessions with individual students.

Chapter 8

MATERIALS, ASSESSMENT, PLANNING

There are some who feel that no real learning can take place unless the teacher and the students have textbooks to read from and refer to. That is not necessarily so. Texts can be important, especially as a guide to the teacher, but they are nothing more nor less than a special kind of resource—a teaching aid that is useful under some circumstances. But there are many different kinds of teaching aids besides texts.

If you are tutoring children, they will undoubtedly bring their school books to your sessions. There is nothing wrong with helping them to use those books, but it will be a waste of the students' time, and yours as well, if you plan your sessions completely around their texts or around what is happening in their classrooms. Your function should not be primarily that of a homework helper. What you ought to want to do is give your students the ability to function in their classrooms without the need of a crutch—such as a tutor—to help them with their homework. This means tapping in to a different set of your student's personal resources than those on which their school teachers are relying.

As we mentioned above, today we have a large variety of enrichment materials, besides textbooks, which are excellent teaching aids. They are available to us in the form of audio and visual tapes, television programs, computer software, pictures, magazines and trade books. But even these have their limits.

One of the most important and positive aspects of the tutoring situation is the relationship that develops between the tutor and the student. The way the student feels about learning, the attitude he or she develops toward the progress being made in the tutoring sessions, will often be the most vital of the determining factors in the amount of effort the student is willing to put into learning. It is that student effort which will produce the big learning payoff, not the texts, tapes or other varieties of software. And it will be the tutor's ability to stimulate an otherwise lethargic or negative student that will determine whether he or she will be learning.

Nevertheless, the software is available and it can often serve as reference material, and sometimes even as motivation, helping to vitalize sessions for the student and to stimulate new ideas for the tutor. Therefore, it is important to know where such materials can be found readily.

Obtaining And Creating Tutoring Materials

There are enormous numbers of catalogs of books and materials suitable for teaching purposes. And there are any number of stores which carry instructional materials for children and adults. Such materials can also be found in the community colleges and in the public school libraries across the country.

The best place to begin to find references is in local public school libraries. If you do not find what it is that you are looking for there, the public library will often be just as helpful. The reference librarian in these institutions is the person to see. He or she will usually be willing to spend time with you helping you locate the particular kinds of materials you think you need.

If you are planning to ask for the assistance of a librarian, be sure to take with you a well thought through list of exactly what kinds of books, magazines, tapes, etc., you are interested in finding. Preparing in advance in this way will help you make the best use of both the librarian's and your own time and will insure that your trip will not have been wasted.

You may also feel that you want to take, or send, your students to the public library so they may find books and reference materials for themselves. It is a good idea to get them involved in this way. One of the most important skills you can provide for your students, one that will serve them well for the rest of their lives, is how to find their way around a public library. You should try to schedule one or two sessions in the library so you can, together, go through the title and author files and the stacks. You should demonstrate the use of a reader's guide, an atlas, an encyclopedia, a dictionary, an almanac, a thesaurus. You should explain and illustrate the use of the decimal system for shelving books. And you should teach how to access a data bank with a computer modem. Basic lessons such as these will serve your students well in seeking information all through their futures.

If you do take students to the library, it would be a good idea to call the librarian in advance and discuss what kind of assistance she or he can offer when you come. Calling in advance and making an appointment will give the librarian a chance to set aside some time for you and to make some notes about the information to be shared. With the librarian's help you will find that there are many instructional magazines available which have practical, easy-to-follow suggestions for finding and creating useful teaching materials. After examining some of these, you may decide that you would like to have your own copies of such periodicals. Subscriptions are generally available.

A caution is in order here. Remember what we have been pointing out all through this book: your students are likely to have rejected the ordinary classroom teaching methods and may need entirely different approaches if they are going to learn. What you find in standard teacher's references may not work with those you are tutoring. Experiment. Trial and error may have to serve you for a while. But, this is where your own creativity can be of utmost importance. Try to take advantage of what you have learned about your students' interests and learning styles. Refer back to their self-assessments. Review what they have told you about their interests. And then, use and build on what seems to work best with them.

Make up games, hunting assignments, reference tasks, a variety of challenges which your students can face and conquer. You may even find it useful to have them create some of their own materials. On some occasions you might even want them to suggest their own assignments. Accept their suggestions and do everything you can to keep their interest high. But make sure that you build success into any assignments you give. Wherever possible, avoid material that is so difficult it will be bound to lead to student failure.

Of course, if you are working on specialty subjects in areas having nothing to do with academics or remediation—things like sewing, ceramics, carpentry or the like—your problems will be different.

To provide instruction in these skills you will need to have a well-equipped studio or workshop as a teaching room. You will also need enough tools and materials for students to use when they come for the first time. In classes such as these it is usually expected that the students will purchase their own materials but that they will use available tools (yours) at least initially. As they become more interested and more competent, they will probably want to own their own tools as well as materials. When this happens, they are likely to ask you to assist them in making purchasing choices. It would be helpful to have a variety of catalogs on hand or know where to send students to refer to such catalogs.

Safety

Because of the obvious dangers inherent in working with tools, both hand tools and power tools, all workshop and studio classes ought to begin with specific lessons devoted to shop-safety rules. These lessons should include:

- Demonstrations and practice in how to hold, carry, manage, turn on, use, turn off, put down, clean and replace parts in the tools and equipment in both your shop and their own;
- Periodic review and strict adherence to all appropriate safety regulations;
- Review of all first-aid procedures and location of all first-aid materials;
- Review of proper methods for cleaning and storage of tools and materials.

Even if your students feel that reviewing the rules is elementary and that it seems to them like a waste of time, do not take it for granted that they know these basics. Review them. Hold safety drills—often. It pays to be as careful as possible when working in a shop of any sort, especially if any of the materials you use are combustible or any of the tools are power-driven.

Mapping Progress

Just as it is important for you to create materials which match the learning styles of your students, so it is important that each of your students be helped to recognize and believe in the fact that he or she really is learning—that real progress is being made at each session.

To help students see this, a graph, a chart, a running assessment page in their notebooks, or some other tangible measure of progress ought to be kept and referred to sometime during each session. Such a graphic display is often a morale booster, even for those who learn easily. In addition, you should regularly accumulate evidence of what your students have learned in your tutoring sessions and encourage them to do the same. Spend a bit of time in an effort to determine what has and hasn't worked and share this information with them. Your students should be helped to understand what their learning styles are—what types of things they learn easily and why, what they struggle to learn and why.

Be sure to include in your tutoring plans for each session an encouraging exercise or some **believable** words of praise for the student's performance. Your clients, especially those who are seeing you for remediation, have heard enough negative comments about their learning. They don't need more of them. They need praise and regular pats on the back for their effort. But be careful. Most students, particularly those who have regularly failed in the past, are likely to be sensitive and quick to pick up on phony praise. Teach yourself to find something to say that is both positive and true. All of us feed on praise, even those who seem to succeed with ease, but we do not like to feel we are being patronized or praised for an unworthy performance.

Periodically, after about the fourth, then the eighth, then the twelfth month, you might wish to review with your students the self-assessment sheet you developed together. It is bound to be enlightening for you both to see what still applies and what has changed. Whenever you do such a review, you will find it valuable to discuss the "why's" and the "how's" of changes which have occurred. Try to learn from your students how they feel about the changes. The student's views ought to be of particular interest to you and you ought to note their comments for use in future review sessions.

If you are working with school-aged students, you will want to plan to have reporting sessions for the parents as well. Consult your students about whether or not they would like to be at these sessions. Only in rare instances should you report to parents without the students present if they wish to be there.

Developing Good Study Habits

What will serve all students well, adults and children, in all areas of academic work, will be improvement in study habits. Many people find it difficult to get themselves to sit down to study. Many also find, even if they have made it to the point of opening a book or notebook, that they get drowsy and tend to want to fall asleep. These are realities and have to be dealt with. The following are some suggestions you may wish to share with your students:

1. Studying is hard work. That has to be admitted. Like all hard work, when we do it well, we get a lot of good feeling from it.

2. Thinking about how much we would like to do it well and be praised for it will help us get to it and stay with it.

3. Anything that takes our attention away from what we are studying makes it harder for us to learn. The radio, TV, family conversations, telephone calls, all pull attention away from what we are doing and that makes learning very much harder.

4. Sitting down to study after a big meal will have us fighting off sleep. Don't get right to it immediately after a big dinner; wait for about an hour.

5. It is a great help to have a notebook and a pencil at hand when reading or when trying to learn something new.

   • If there is a word we don't know or an idea we don't understand, or something we want to be sure to remember, it is easy to jot down the page and line where it can be found, and sometimes even write a note to ourselves about just what it is we want to remember.

   • That makes it possible to share it, review it, or get some help with finding solutions and answers in the next tutoring session.

   • A notebook is for keeping notes. These may be notes to ourselves or for ourselves or for sharing with someone else. We should organize the notebook so that it will be easy to locate what we wish to refer to in the future.

   • A notebook can be used as an extension of our memory and can help to keep us from worrying about whether we might forget something we especially want to remember.

   • It is a good idea to look through the notebook we are keeping, regularly, to be sure there is nothing in it which we haven't resolved.

6. All assignments are to be done. That is our obligation to ourselves, not to anyone else.

   • Assignments are given so that we can work on developing and fixing our skills.

   • If we don't do those assignments, we are not failing anyone but ourselves.

   • All assignments given in our tutoring sessions will be examined, reviewed together, critiqued and evaluated.

7. Some things to be learned are skills. To learn a skill, practice is necessary. Writing and spelling are skills. Taking tests is a skill. If we wish to become good at a skill, we must practice it with as much

attention and concentration as most athletes devote to practicing a sport.

8. Reading is a very complex skill. It needs even more practice than most sports because it involves a whole set of accomplishments, including the ability to: "see," "hear," "think," "speak," "imagine," "solve puzzles," "organize," "conclude," "make judgments."

9. Reading is a skill with an enormous payoff, because once we have mastered it, it is ours for the rest of our lives.

It is important that you try to convince your students that when they are stuck on something, even if they have been helped on that very same thing many times before, they should feel free to tell you about the trouble they are having. You should encourage them to come to you for assistance without feeling shy or self-conscious about it. You should help your students to believe that having difficulty is not a sin. Nor should they be thinking that they are "stupid" just because they are finding it hard to learn something. If they can't "get" what they are trying to learn, convince them that you will help them find another way to learn it.

The above comments concerning study habits are not only valid for remedial students. They apply equally well to all students, even those who come to you for instruction in how to play games.

Planning And Preparation For Each Session

You can count on the fact that the students you tutor are going to be especially sensitive to what you do and how you do it. Again, this applies not only to those seeking remediation but to anyone paying you to help them learn something. If you are not well prepared for a session, if you are "winging it," they will know it and their response is almost guaranteed to be negative.

It is vital that you take the time to plan and prepare for each session.

- Have the materials you wish to use ready.
- Review the contents of the student's folder so that you are conversant with what has gone on at previous sessions and are ready to take up where you have left off and move on.
- Have the corrected student work ready to return and be discussed.
- Be as single-purposed and interested as possible so that you can convince your students that they are not only important to you during a tutoring session but you consider them important enough

(even when they are not actually present) to think about and plan for.

This reassurance is especially needed if you are working on remediation. Remember that many of those who seek remedial tutoring have self-esteem problems as a result of repeated previous failures. Too often they can't believe they matter enough for anyone to devote much effort to them. A good tutor has an opportunity to dispel that negative self-image and make them feel better about themselves.

The best time to plan for the next session is in those few moments immediately after the student leaves. This is when his or her successes, failures and learning needs are freshest in your mind. A handy way to plan is to jot notes to yourself about what you wish to do at the following session and attach these to the outside of the individual's record folder. Then when you are ready to see the student again, the plan will be right there waiting for you. A suggested lesson plan form is provided in Appendix F. Feel free to tear it out and reproduce it as often as you like.

You will find that well-planned sessions are easier to conduct and yield much greater satisfaction than those which are not planned at all, or are poorly planned, primarily because the results in student performance are bound to be better.

Chapter 9

TUTORING READING

With so many people in the country unable to read, one of the major markets for professional tutors today is in the area of reading. This chapter and the next will be devoted to suggested approaches in working as a tutor for the reading-handicapped, including the functionally illiterate, both children and adults.

It is easy to imagine how difficult it is for an adult who cannot read to get along in the modern world where so much of what one does takes a person's ability to read for granted. But think of how much worse it would be to be a student in a classroom in which reading is central to almost all other learning and not be able to make sense of the symbols that are supposed to be telling you what to do and how to do it. Can you picture the desperation you would soon be feeling? "Something has gone wrong. It seems that everyone else catches on but me," the non-reader thinks. "I must be very stupid." Imagine how it feels to have lived with that thought for years, and imagine how much worse it would be if you were really very bright but had a physical impairment that kept you from being able to see properly. Sometimes (not always) the inability to learn to read can be traced to a vision problem.

A Discussion Of Methods

There are probably as many ways of teaching reading as there are highways in this country. Each method has advocates ready to defend "a" way as "the" way. Many "How To..." books have been written on the subject over the years and there are experts everywhere, ready to advise anyone willing to listen on how one should teach reading.

The argument is irrelevant for you as a tutor. How you teach is not the issue. The widest possible choices are available and the most eclectic approaches will probably serve you best. However, no matter how you choose to proceed, it will not matter a whit unless your students are learning. Those who have sat in dozens of classrooms over the years and failed to learn are proof of that. And since whether or not your students are learning is the only issue that is important in a tutoring situation, it is your responsibility as a tutor to plan your lessons in such a way that you do a minimum of presenting and your students do a maximum of doing: seeking, trying, practicing and, of course, learning. This kind of approach should apply whether you are working with adults or children. Always keep your focus on what your students are learning rather than on what you are teaching.

Before you begin working with your non-reading students, whether they are adults or children, it is important that you ask them to visit a competent opthalmologist. Some of your students may be suffering from "dyslexia," a term given to a complex of physical visual difficulties causing a variety of problems for those who suffer with it. Some forms of dyslexia can be controlled with special lenses. Others cannot. Dyslexic students need patient, understanding handling, since they are always grappling with distorted vision. The eye doctor may be able to treat the student's optical problems while you are working on the learning problem. Then again, treatment may not help. Nor can we count on dyslexia disappearing with age. The best thing we can do for such students is recognize, and help them recognize, the problems they are having and then to aid them in finding ways to cope.

Specific strategies, including framing words, mirror techniques, repetition, multi-sensual experiences, and many, many others can be found in the myriad of books on teaching the dyslexic. Such books can be borrowed from college and university libraries. But even with these books in hand, you may still have to search out what will work for the individual you have as a student. The problem he or she suffers with may be unique and call for a unique set of methods. Searching out what will work may take time and patience. Most students, however, will not be that difficult to tutor.

One very simple but very practical suggestion for all students is that they always come to sessions with a notebook, a pen and a pencil. This will help both them and you in the learning process.

Alphabet

An important basic for all who are trying to learn to read, both adults and children, is a solid knowledge of the alphabet. Your students should know how to read it, write it and recite it, and they should be aware of its power in our language.

- The letters and their positions on paper are what makes it possible for us to read, to write and to understand messages.
- Those twenty-six alphabet letters stand for all of the forty-five English language sounds we make when we talk to each other.
- The letters are actually symbols which we use when we write.
- They are the building blocks of our oral and written communication system.
- Because of the alphabet we can record our experiences and our history, as well as the history of our planet, our solar system and our universe.
- The alphabet enables us to accumulate and build on knowledge; scientific advances would be impossible if we had no way to note and pass on from one generation to the next what we learn through experimentation.
- Because of the alphabet we can share our speculations about the future.
- Alphabet letters are the single greatest help to us in organizing our knowledge and in allowing us to store, access and retrieve information.

Some of your early tutoring sessions with every student ought to be devoted to work on learning the alphabet. Your students may scoff and be resistant to such lessons at first, thinking that they are too elementary to bother with, but you will be amazed to find out how little some of them know about how to use those twenty-six letters. Even if they are able to recite them, they will not necessarily be able to name the letters if they appear out of the expected alphabetical order, nor know the sounds the letters make even if they can name them, nor be able to match the small and the capital letters.

There are a few suggestions offered below for helping students fix alphabetical knowledge. You will undoubtedly have many additional ideas. Use them.

Oral Exercises For Students

1. Memorize alphabet songs ("A—You're Adorable...."; "I Got A Gal In Kalamazoo")

2. Recite five letters at a time forward and backward (klmno-onmlk; pqrst-tsrqp)
3. Recite the entire alphabet forward and backward;
4. Fill in the missing letters (b, c, __, e, __, __, h; L, __, __, O, __, __, R) in both upper and lower case.
5. Use a variety of alphabet games such as: "My name is Adam," "Going to Jerusalem" (see Appendix G);
6. Mouth the consonant sounds of each of the letters and use a hand mirror to see what happens to your mouth;
7. Mouth the various vowel sounds; watch the configurations of your mouth as you do this;
8. Combine various consonant and vowel sounds;
9. Discuss the function of vowels and consonants in the English language;
10. Examine and pronounce diphthongs;
11. Name the letters and mouth their sounds—use both small and capital letters not in alphabetical order;
12. Discuss the proper use of capitals and small letters.
13. Using the exercises in Appendix G as models, create a variety of additional challenges for your students.

Research (Finding) Exercises

1. Have students mark all of a particular letter found in a newspaper or magazine article whether those letters occur at the beginning, the end, or elsewhere in a word, whether or not they appear as capital letters;
2. Using two columns in the front page of a newspaper, have students make three lists: the first of all words they find beginning with "r"; the second of all words beginning with "s"; the third of all words beginning with "t" (small letters only; vary the letters).
3. Have students arrange anagram or other block letters in ascending and descending alphabetical order; arrange them skipping a letter; skipping a letter backwards;
4. With material you have prepared, have students alphabetize on the second letter in a list of words or sounds. (For this you will have to have made cardboard tiles with a first and second letter on each—ca, ce, ch, ci, cl, co, cr, cu, cy, cz. (Note: use only letter

combinations possible at the beginning of standard English words or the words themselves.)

5. As students become more competent in handling these exercises, go ahead and have them alphabetize on the third letter;
6. Have students find a series of words in a dictionary, in a thesaurus, in an encyclopedia. (Even if they cannot read or understand the meaning, they can practice finding the word.)

Typewriter Or Computer Keyboard Exercises

1. Have students name and then type each of the letters as they appear on a standard keyboard; have them note the difference between how they look on the keys (capitals) and how they look as they are typed out.
2. At your direction, have the students find and type each of the letters both as capitals and as small letters;
3. Have students type the letters in alphabetical order, then in reverse alphabetical order;
4. Give students several special combinations of letters to type;
5. Have students type their names; your name;
6. Give students simple sentences to copy (after they have read the sentences) and have them read them again after they are typed;
7. Give students word families to type and read (and, band, bland, brand, gland, grand, hand, land, sand, stand);
8. Have students dictate some simple sentences to you, and after you write them, have them copy what you have written with the typewriter and then read what they have typed;
9. Give students their typed pages to paste into their notebooks.

Spelling Exercises

1. Begin to practice spelling skills by having students read off each of the letters in their sight words (see a following section "Whole Word Recognition");
2. Have students type these words, first by copying them and then from memory;
   • Immediately after typing each word have them compare their output with the word as it appears on their flash card, checking letter by letter;

- Help students to make any corrections that might be necessary;
3. Teach appropriate spelling rules as you proceed. Helpful spelling rules will be found in the grammar books cited in the bibliography as well as in most sixth grade spellers.
4. Have students copy spelling rules (no more than one or two at any session) into their notebooks.
5. Encourage students to memorize these rules. They will be very helpful all through life.

Handwriting Exercises

1. Every student ought to have a practice assignment to write individual letters of the alphabet in their lower case and capital forms as part of their homework assignment after each session;
2. Plan to have some writing practice take place during the tutoring session as well;
   - It should be devoted to correct formation of letters and letter combinations;
   - If students find handwriting particularly difficult, have them concentrate on fewer letters at a sitting (even as few as one at a time) and devote more time to each sitting;
   - Give students the opportunity to write letters in the air, on a newsprint pad on an easle, in a box of sand; have them form letters from clay strips.

Students should be helped to understand that even though we now have portable keyboards, there are occasions when each of us is expected to be able to write (taking notes, leaving a written message, signing our names, filling out applications, completing a form in a doctor's office). We never know when we are going to be called upon to do one of these things. Because this is so, our handwriting must be legible.

Creative Writing And Formal Writing

As part of any good reading lesson, a tutor ought to encourage students to do some creative writing so that they may express ideas, tell stories, seek or share information, and even keep records. Students may resist writing assignments at first. People who read poorly are all too often convinced that they have to be incompetent writers as well. They are afraid to try.

Your role as a tutor should be to provide writing exercises which are within the capability of a handicapped student, starting with very easy assignments (write a sentence telling what the color of this pencil is) and increasing the difficulty of such assignments very slowly. All student writing should be reviewed with the student and helpful comments should be offered both orally and in writing. Some suggested assignments can be found in the Appendix H.

Whole-Word Recognition

One of the classic methods of teaching reading is to have students become familiar with whole words, learn their configurations and be able to recognize them in the same way we recognize the faces of people we know. For some, this method works. For many it works only partially. In the long run, we are not able to rely completely on memorizing whole words. There are just too many of them. We learn to move from whole word recognition to decoding skills at some point. But in the beginning, recognizing some words as familiar units (sight words) can be very useful and flash cards can help in that recognition process.

Commercial flash cards can be purchased, but you would probably be better advised to make your own. Then you can vary the words on the cards to conform with the reading materials your individual students are working on. Vary the size of the card to suit the particular needs of your students. Index card size (or even half of that) may be appropriate for some adults. For children you may prefer to use something larger. A package of stiff cardboard or oaktag can be bought in the notions department of many different kinds of stores, and these sheets can be cut to any size you think is comfortable to handle. Old file folders can be cut down. A black felt-tip pen is useful for making the letters stand out well. You might wish to use both capital and small letters on these cards and to use both sides of the cards.

Remember, when working with your students who have almost certainly experienced a great deal of failure in the past, encouragement and rewards are especially important as they begin to learn. Flash card exercises provide excellent opportunities for praise and rewards.

Flash card words are also useful for the construction of sentences. They can be moved about easily and combined in various ways. Students should be given every opportunity to do this, even to make up absurd sentences. In addition, there are many interesting games (for both adults and children) that can be played with flash cards. Teacher's magazines are full of them.

Once students are able to recognize a flash card word every time they see it, that flash card should become their property. (Each student should have his or her own set.) Even after students have earned their sight words, periodic review of the flash cards should take place. As the student's stack of cards grows, it provides very tangible evidence of the learning that has taken place.

Some additional exercises your students can work on might be:

- Having them find and underline their flash card words in newspaper or magazine articles;
- Having them type and read the words either from the computer screen or from the typewriter paper;
- Having them practice writing the words for handwriting homework;
- Having them write simple sentences using one or more of the words in each sentence;
- Having them find each of the flash card words in the dictionary.

Phonetics—Encoding And Decoding

The major purpose of a phonetic approach to teaching reading is to give students the opportunity to learn to recognize and use sound combinations. Working with the alphabet, students learned that letters and combinations of those letters stand for sounds. Now it is important for them to learn that the placement of these letters and letter combinations at the beginning, in the middle and at the end of other letters and combinations of letters is how words are constructed and how we are able to sound-out unfamiliar words. They must begin to become familiar with:

- All the possible consonant combinations found not only at the beginning of a word but anywhere in a word (br, tr, fl, ck, etc.);
- The possible vowel combinations (dipthongs—au, ou, ae, io, ai, etc.);
- Mixed consonant-vowel combinations (ing, ate, tion, est, etc.);
- All kinds of affixes—prefixes, suffixes, phonemes, morphemes.

And they must begin to work on developing the ability to put various combinations of these together to make words. The process is called encoding. This encoding ability is what we are striving to develop when we ask students to learn word families. Once a student recognizes "it" and knows the sounds of the letters of the alphabet, putting an "s" in front of "it" to make "sit" begins to make sense. Often, students seem to catch on to encoding and can build word families as long as we stick to one base word. But if we move from "it" to "and," some find it quite difficult to generalize their experience without assistance. Patience and repetition are absolutely necessary in helping students learn these skills.

Just as students learn to build words through encoding, they also have to learn to break words down by decoding. They can be helped to do this if you guide them to find the base words and the letter combinations they are familiar with in unknown words, especially in those daunting "big" words, and help them sound them out (ex-tra-or-di-nary).

Applying learning from one situation to another is often harder for the student than we believe it should be. It can take some of them a very long time, as well as a great deal of experience, before they are able, with confidence, to use the encoding and decoding processes in more than the particular instances they have practiced.

Again it must be stressed that you, as a tutor, must have infinite patience. What seems so obvious to you may not "click" for your students until they have tried it again and again. For some, a constant repetition is necessary before learning is fixed. This is especially true of "slow learners." Those who are slow to learn are usually slow to generalize as well. As a tutor you should always keep in mind that slow learners learn more slowly, but they do learn.

Once students are able to generalize from the specific sound combinations they have learned, they will have just about mastered encoding and decoding—which are two of the key processes in learning to read. The skill will become fixed as your students continue to read.

You will find a complete citation in the Bibliography for an excellent book which is a very helpful teaching tool. It is called *The Reading Teacher's Book of Lists* and contains all kinds of lists of words categorized for all kinds of purposes.

That reading will make them better readers is the next most important lesson for newly empowered readers to learn. Like with any other skill, it is practice that keeps us in shape. Only continuing to spend time reading can make readers of us. To read well and enjoy what we are reading, we must read a lot.

Chapter 10

TUTORING READING—ADDITIONAL COMMENTS

The English language is renowned for being inconsistent. Just when students seem to have things under control, they start to make some funny discoveries. For example:

- Take the word "ghiti." Doesn't it spell FISH? It would if English were consistent. The "gh" would sound like "f" as in "tough"—the "ti" would sound like "sh" as in "motion."
- Take the word "phlass." Is it possible that that would be FLASH? The "ph" would be sounded as "f" as in the word "phone"—the "ss" would be sounded "sh" as in the word "mission."
- Look at the spelling of the words "table" and "label."
- Look at the pronunciation of the words "read" (present tense) and "read" (past tense).

Those are only a very few examples of hundreds of inconsistencies which can be found. The English language is full of them. You and your students could make long lists of them. In fact, it would be a good idea to create such lists, adding to them each time you come across additional examples of inconsistencies. It would be one way of turning what might otherwise be a discouraging hassle, a labyrinth of challenges, into a game.

Because of these multitudes of inconsistencies which are constantly cropping up to destroy all semblance of neat patterns, encoding and decoding skills are absolutely vital to the reader. They ought to be practiced regularly. Encoding and decoding are what almost all competent readers rely on when they are faced with unfamiliar words.

But as we have already stated, not everyone will find it easy to understand the workings of these two processes. If your students cannot seem to catch on to what you are trying to help them learn, there is no sense at all in haranguing them. Whether they are adults or children, pressure has not yet helped them learn and probably never will. Be patient. Try more sight words in families. Stay alert for clues from them about what they have learned—and keep trying.

The Right Method

Once again it must be stressed that there is no right method for teaching reading. If there were, no student would need tutoring. Therefore, it will be up to you as you tutor to match method and student. It will be up to you to vary methods when it seems appropriate to do so and to resist the temptation to introduce variation when what you have been doing is working. The one thing you can absolutely rely on is that the more the students are expected to do for themselves in "hands-on" situations, the more and the faster they will learn and the more firmly that learning will be internalized.

As you work with students, your experience will tell you that varying what you do together in your sessions will keep some students interested and vitalize the sessions for them, but will cause others to become nervous. Some learners rely on sameness, others can't stand it. You have to understand the needs of each of your students and respond appropriately to those needs if you are going to be successful in getting them to learn when many have failed with them before.

Don't be afraid of repetition. If it seems boring to you, think of it as what it actually is—practice. You may not need it, but your students do. All skills, both physical and mental, call for rigorous practice if they are to be mastered.

Consider the fact that the students who have come to you for help may be suffering from a variety of disorders which may never have been precisely identified. Identifying them may be among the earliest steps you have to take. Using pertinent remedial approaches would follow.

Identifying Problems

We have already spoken about the possibility that your student might be suffering from dyslexia. This is a specific term used to describe a spectrum of conditions. Some have to do with how the eye handles light and dark contrasts. Some have to do with eye-brain coordination. Some have to do with hormonal or nutritional deficiencies of one sort or another. And some are so difficult to diagnose that no one knows what the cause or causes may be. Besides the general term, dyslexia, there are all kinds of words used to identify potential conditions the student may be suffering from.

- Perseveration—the inability to shift comfortably from one word to another or from one activity to another.
- Mixed Dominance and Ambidexterity—the reliance on the right hand to do some things and the left to do others (often leading to confusion).
- Reversals and Inversions—the students see and reproduce some words and some letters backwards or upside down and think they have done the exercises correctly.
- Extreme Distractability—the student's attention span is minimal and he or she finds it difficult to sustain concentration.

Although the troubles are different, the approaches a tutor can use in dealing with all of these difficulties is similar:

- Have the student (adult or child) see a doctor for identification and treatment of any physically treatable difficulties.
- Watch closely as the student reads and writes to determine exactly what the difficulty seems to be and how they react to it.
- Encourage the students to verbalize and describe to you the kind of trouble they are having. Believe their descriptions. (They may have spoken to others in the past and not been believed.)
- Use a great deal of repetition in your sessions and encourage the students to do the major part of the repeating.
- Have students involved as active participants rather than as passive receptors in all lessons.

The following are a few examples of exercises which may be helpful. Teacher's libraries have volumes of additional materials. Find ideas and adapt them to your needs.

1. For those who reverse letters (*was* for *saw*):
   - Have student trace the initial letter with a fingertip (or color the first letter), make the sound of the letter, then say the word.
   - Have students circle all words which are alike on a line: was was saw ash has was awe caw was maw
   - Using flash cards, have students match cards from a pile of look-alikes and trace and sound the first letter.
2. For students who confuse letters (b and d; h and n; q and g; m and w; etc.):

- Use various exercises matching listed letters to words.
- Using newspapers have students circle each "b" and underline each "d"; etc.
- Leave the first letter blank in a list of words. Have students insert letter and read word: __ ake b,c,f,l,m,r,s,t,w,; __ ell b,d,f,g,h, j,s,t,w,y
- Leave the final letter blank on a list of words and have the student insert the letter and read the words. bo __ b,g,n,o,p,w,x,y, pa __ d,l,n,p,r,t,w,x,y

3. For students who find it difficult to focus:
   - Have students use two hands to frame a difficult word blocking out all others in the sentence.
   - Have student use a finger to point to words and letters.

There are dozens of other exercises which will help and they are available in schools and libraries.

Remember that your students themselves will be a good source for suggesting things they like to do. If they are doing what they enjoy doing, a part of the battle will have been won.

Reading Silently—Reading Aloud

There was at one time a great deal of controversy over whether students ought to be taught to read aloud or to read silently. The best advice is to have students practice reading both ways. Each is actually a separate skill and contributes to the facility with which the student is eventually able to do the other. When your purpose is to check student pronunciation and ability to decipher unfamiliar words, or to have the student share something with you or others, reading aloud is vital. When you are after speed and comprehension, or enjoyment of content, silent reading is what you should ask for.

Reading Aloud

One of the rewards of skillful reading is being able to present something (read) to other people. To do this, students must learn skills needed for reading aloud with competence. To read aloud effectively, the reader must sound as much as possible as though he or she is talking. This means that the eyes have to scan a few words, or a phrase, or even a complete sentence ahead, while the reader recites what has just been scanned. This is not easy to do until it has been practiced many times. In addition to scanning ahead, the eyes must be raised from the page at fairly frequent intervals to make contact with the people who are listening. The several skills involved in doing this are not easy to acquire, but they are worth having and, therefore, worth practicing.

As a tutor you can help students learn to read aloud by presenting, and then removing from view, short phrases, asking the students to say what they saw when they can no longer see it. At first they may be totally unable or unwilling even to try to do this. Stick with it. Encourage them to try. As they increase their ability and succeed a few times, you can introduce longer and more complex phrases. For example:

- First exercises—ran, jumped, sat, the, president, walked, ate (familiar individual nouns, verbs and articles presented to the student and then hidden before the student "reads" them aloud).
- Second series of exercises—He ran. She jumped. The dog sat. See the president. We ate. (Use two- to three-word combinations and the very same show-and-hide process used with single words.)
- Third series of exercises—Send the boy—to the store—to buy—milk for the family. (Use phrases from a sentence and entire short sentences from a paragraph with the same show, hide and recite process.)

In these kinds of exercises your emphasis has to be on having the phrase make sense to the ear of the listener. That can't happen if the student recites the phrase word by word. Putting "expression" into the recitation is the same as giving it meaning. Your example, showing how it ought to be done, will be most important. This is one time when you would be correct to impose a standard on your students, both on the children and the adults, and help them to rise to it.

Reading good literature to your students in a competent and entertaining manner is another very good idea. It serves both as a demonstration and an inspiration, and, as they become interested in the plots of the stories you read to them, it can serve as a way to motivate students to want to read more themselves. After a while you might begin to take turns in reading paragraphs aloud. When they are finally able to participate in this way in a reading lesson, be sure to praise them and help them see how much they have progressed.

Reading Silently (For A Purpose)

Generally when students are reading silently, they are reading for a purpose. The purposes may be very different each time they approach printed matter, and even some of the skills they need to use may vary, but the purpose is there.

We have spent a great deal of time in discussions about the mechanics of learning to read. But, although mastery of the techniques and skills of reading is a first, and a vital step that a tutor must attend to in helping students master the hierarchy of skills a competent reader needs, the real importance of reading has much less to do with process and much more to do with entry into the world of knowledge.

Most of us read to obtain information. It is something we do automatically all of the time. We read a menu to find out what a restaurant is serving; we read a street sign to know where we are; we read a manual to learn how to repair something; we read a recipe book to learn how to prepare food; we read a table of contents to see what is in a book; we read a dictionary definition to find out what a word means.

There are some students who have learned some of the mechanics of reading but can't seem to make much sense of the sounds they are making. They are stuck at a primitive stage. They have not learned to read for information or for meaning. They have merely acquired some of the decoding skills. If you recognize that this has happened to one of your students, it is time to devote both your efforts and those of your student to deciphering what is being said. The student will have to:

- Practice reading silently in phrases;
- Stop after one or two phrases to talk about what was said; you should help if they cannot tell, and then have them reread;
- Work hard on vocabulary development, recognizing both the sound and the meaning of words. (In Appendix I, you will find a functional reading word list for adults which will be helpful to you and your students.)
- Practice matching sentences to pictures;
- Practice using words correctly in sentences;
- Practice recalling the sequence of events occurring in a story (begin with two incidents, then three, etc.);
- Tell why events took place in a specific order;
- Tell a story;
- Learn to identify the central meaning of a paragraph or a chapter;

- Recount the action that is taking place;
- Identify characters and tell what they do in the story.

You might also introduce a silent reading selection with two or three questions you want the students to find answers to while they are reading. If they miss the answers, help them go back and find them.

You and your students working together ought to devise interesting exercises which will help them develop and internalize these skills. You might also wish to obtain a copy of an exercise book developed for use with students learning English as a second language. It is a book of sequences of cartoon drawings with empty "balloons" over the heads of the characters, allowing you and your students to fill in the conversations. The book is called, *Lexicary, An Illustrated Vocabulary Builder for Second Languages,* and is fully cited in the Bibliography at the back of this manual.

When students are reading for information they should be encouraged to let their eyes scan sentences as quickly as possible rather than to stop to digest every word. The mind can accumulate data much more quickly in sentences and phrases than in individual words. (This is the reason speed-reading works as well as it does.) Once the gist of the content is discovered, the students can return to specific parts of the passage, to particular words or sentences to check the information they have gleaned. Scanning is an important reading skill and should be practiced along with the rest of the reading skills the students are learning to use.

Of course, one of the most rewarding aspects of reading is being able to read for pleasure and for the satisfaction of personal curiosity. Story books, novels, mysteries, histories, all are engrossing and have the ability to transport us out of ourselves, out of our mundane lives into other times, other places, even other worlds. We also read for the purpose of enjoying an artistic experience. Along with the story, we can begin to appreciate the beauty of our language and the power of what it is able to do by stimulating our imagination and helping us to respond to the word-pictures being painted.

We can only read what someone has written, so we might say that writing is the other side of reading. To write, we not only have to know how to form letters but how to spell words and choose from among them the ones we want to use. After that we have to put them together in sentences that make sense. If we don't spell well or write legibly, whatever it was that we wanted to say will not be readable by anyone else.

We rely on standard patterns of spelling and writing for accurate communication. Students must be helped to appreciate this message. It is why learning to spell accurately is so important, especially in English where so many words would change their meaning completely with the addition or removal of a single letter—even if that letter is silent. Think of the difference between the words "sing" and "singe."

A singular gift you can give your students, as we have already claimed in a previous chapter, is membership in a local public library. Offer to meet them there and to help them join. Then, take them on a tour of the shelves and assist them in choosing their first books. Also, conduct the library lessons outlined in Chapter 8. Newspapers, textbooks, literature, science, the arts, and religion are just a few of the things that open up for your students when they conquer their handicap of not being able to read. Once they have learned, they will be able to use a variety of reference materials to learn even more.

Most students will realize that there is a great deal more for them to know, but some will have a tendency to want to quit learning as soon as they have acquired a small amount of proficiency. Try to hold on to them until they can really enjoy a good book, really get the essence of a magazine or newspaper story. In the long run they will thank you for it.

You can count on the fact that if you present students with learning materials and situations which reflect their interests, they will be more motivated to learn than if you use standard teaching materials. Textbooks are fine as guides for you, but they tend to turn the student off. Whenever possible, tap into the enormous amount of reading material available which is not textual. Both you and your students should collect materials which reflect their interests and use these in tutoring sessions.

The most important thing to remember to share with your students is what we said before—to read well a person must read, and the more one reads, the more one will enjoy reading. Thus, it goes almost without saying that the room in which you tutor should have at least one good-sized bookcase filled with a variety of attractive books, magazines and other reading material. You should be willing to lend these to your students (one book at a time) and should be ready to talk about each of these books with them when they are returned.

Don't forget to take time to evaluate student progress. Be encouraging and supportive. That will pay dividends in better student work.

Chapter 11

TUTORING MATHEMATICS

More than just about any other subject, mathematics, particularly arithmetic, geometry and algebra, which are the areas of math you will most likely be asked to tutor, are built on a step-by-step series of processes. Functioning well on each new step is dependent on knowing how to function on the previous steps. Trying to function in algebra or geometry without understanding why we do what we do in arithmetic will be a task of major difficulty. A strong math base with solid understanding will lead to strong performance skills. A weak or patchy base will result in a "swiss-cheese" knowledge of the subject—one full of unexpected holes. It will, as well, frequently lead to fear of math and the inability to perform even simple math tasks successfully.

Students who have missed the school lessons in which particular processes were presented, or who have failed to master those processes even though they may have been there when they were presented, tend to be "math-handicapped" throughout their lives. When simple concepts haven't "clicked," pushing the student on to where he or she must deal with more complex concepts (as most classroom teachers feel they must do in order to be able to cover the work of the grade) often will increase students' confusion and cause them to despise and reject math. This rejection and math-handicap is almost certain to worsen rather than to cure itself. It gets better only when specific attention is focused on what is wrong and a plan is made and followed for making it right. It is because they hope they will be able to accomplish this "making it right" that people seek tutoring. And if you can provide the help they are looking for, you will be doing them a most remarkable favor.

As in reading, there are many different legitimate approaches to teaching mathematics. The ones advocated here are suggested because they will tend to give the students, adults or children, the firmest base, the maximum support and the maximum understanding of arithmetic and other geometric and algebraic processes by relying heavily on student participation in every facet of the learning and by taking nothing for granted, moving very slowly, and stopping very frequently to check on and review how well the student has learned and has fixed the learning.

Whenever it is at all possible, even though excellent commercial materials are certainly available, your students ought to be encouraged to make or construct their own learning materials. In this way they will be using not just their minds for figuring but their eyes and their hands as well. Bringing as many senses as possible into the learning (a multisensory approach) helps students to grasp concepts and to remember better. When they learn this way they more easily understand the math that is involved and internalize more firmly the ideas and processes you are expecting them to learn.

Just as we started the section on learning to read with the alphabet, so we will start this section on learning math with what is absolutely basic to math—learning the numbers, numerals, counting—and the "tables."

Arithmetic Basics

One of the most stable, the most unvarying set of rules in the world is the set that results in the arithmetic tables. Unless you are working in "other base systems," in which one and one may not add up to the numeral two (although it will always add up to the quantity of two), in the base ten system, which is the major arithmetical system we use in this country, we can rely on one and one always resulting in two. And six and five are always going to result in eleven. And ten times any number will always end in a zero.

The arithmetic tables are also called the number facts, and people who are at ease with math can generally provide immediate response on all of the basic number facts. They are the answers we get when we combine two numbers at a time (and we always combine only two numbers at a time no matter how many will eventually be combined in a single problem) by using them in the four basic arithmetic processes (addition, subtraction, multiplication and division).

Arithmetic is extremely logical. It is easy to tutor if you go slowly and take things step by step. And, once some of the obstacles (especially the students' fear and anxiety of not being able to come up with correct answers) are removed, it is easy to learn. To do both well, some practical materials should always be on hand.

Materials

The materials you will need to tutor successfully include:

- Your two hands and ten fingers and those of your student;
- Eleven pennies, eleven dimes, and at least one dollar bill;
- A bead-board strung with ten rows of ten movable beads on each row (this should be made by the student);
- 100 or more toothpicks, ice-cream sticks, or tongue depressors bundled with rubber bands into bundles of ten; ten loose ones;
- A hand-held calculator;
- A variety of multi-colored poker chips which can represent pennies, dimes and dollars;
- A set of tables for each of the arithmetic processes (We recommend that these be made by you and the student—together—and the method for making them is precisely discussed below and in the Appendixes J and K.)
- Arithmetic texts and workbooks;
- An arithmetic notebook.

First Things First

The very first thing a student has to learn is that the arithmetic number facts must be memorized. No matter how long it takes, this is an exercise which should be given the highest priority even if what you are tutoring is geometry or algebra. All arithmetic is based on knowing those sums, products and differences, and immediate response to number facts is the single most helpful skill a student can develop. Once learned, the number facts give the student math power; unlearned, they are a perpetual source of frustration, embarrassment and worry.

It may seem odd to students who have come to you to be tutored in algebra or geometry that you insist on starting by checking their familiarity with number facts. Don't be put off by that. Nine times out of ten you will find that the student who needs tutoring not only cannot provide immediate response on the number facts but will even provide responses which are not only wrong but also inconsistent. This is an absolute giveaway that they have little understanding of the combinations or the quantities involved. Insisting that your students develop this skill may be the greatest contribution you will be able to make to their functioning as arithmetic-able adults.

Tables

Constructing tables is a first step in learning these number facts and fixing them in memory. Working together, you and your student should begin with two sheets of graph paper that you have ruled to darken the lines. The boxes should be made large enough to enter numbers legibly. The first number fact sheet should be headed ADDITION—SUBTRACTION. The second number fact should be headed MULTI-PLICATION—DIVISION. Using the first sheet (ADDITION—SUBTRACTION), write in the numbers from one to ten across the top and then down the left side. Then help the students fill in the rest of the numbers by adding the top number in any column to the number in the column at the left side and putting the result in the box where the two numbers would meet.

Students can use their fingers or real material to find the answer if they need to. All the boxes should be filled-in in this way. The finished table can be found illustrated in Appendix J. (The logic of the pattern should become apparent to your students very quickly. If it doesn't, help them see it.)

Now help the students see that starting with any number on the top line and adding to it any number on the side line (or vice versa) will give them the sum in the box where the lines cross. (To add we move to the right or down.) Then have them start in any box (where they have entered the addition answers) and by moving up they will find the difference between the number they started with and the number to the left of where they started. By moving left they will find the difference between the number they started with and the number at the top of the column. (Ten in column six is ten minus six; move to the left and see at a glance that the answer is four.) This table will serve as a handy reference for your students and a way to check their answers, but it is not to be considered a substitute for memorizing the addition and subtraction number facts.

The second reference table is headed MULTIPLICATION—DIVISION. To get the most from this table, you should first show your students that multiplication is repeated addition, division is repeated subtraction; show how multiplication can be "undone" by dividing, and division can be "undone" by multiplying. Once these concepts are learned, a table can be constructed.

On the ruled paper headed MULTIPLICATION—DIVISION, write

the numbers from one to twelve across the top and again down the left side. (See the finished table illustrated in Appendix K.) Across the top write the numbers from one to twelve. Down the left side, write the numbers from one to twelve. Now under the number one, have your students think— one taken one time—fill in that number (1) in the box where one and one cross. Move down in the one column to the two box. Have the student think (and use their fingers or manipulative materials to find the answer) one taken two times? Fill in that answer (2) where the one and two cross.

When students use their fingers, beads, toothpicks, sticks or any other available real materials to discover the answers to these number facts, they should begin to see how multiplication works.

Help your students fill in the rest of the table. (Four taken three times is the same as three fours or four threes, and where four and three cross the number twelve should be entered.) This table will assist students as they learn to count by other numbers than one and should help in achieving immediate response on the multiplication and division number facts.

Using the table for division is easy. Find any number in the grid. If we take 18, running our eye up we find the number 6, and running our eye to the left we find the number 3. 18 divided by 6 equals 3. 18 divided by 3 equals 6. (Stress with real materials that "divided by" means separated into that many groups and results in a number of units within each group.)

Again, the table is a handy reference to be used for checking results, but the number facts should be learned—internalized so completely that immediate response becomes almost second nature.

Number Line And Graphics

While you are constructing tables, you should also construct a number line so that students begin to visualize what is meant by positive and negative numbers. This will be especially useful if you are working to help students with algebra and geometry.

Draw a ten-inch line across the paper. In the middle make a jot and label it "0." Then make a jot every half inch in each direction. Label the jots to the right with positive ascending numerals and the jots to the left with negative ascending numerals. A model number line can be found in Appendix J.

The number line is an excellent device for illustrating what happens when positive numbers are added or subtracted, when negative numbers are added or subtracted, or when a positive and negative number are added or subtracted. (Move to the right and count when adding positive numbers; move to the left and count when subtracting positive numbers; move to the left and count when adding negative numbers; move to the right and count when subtracting negative numbers.)

Additional important graphics to have your students construct and cut out are circles, squares, rectangles, and a variety of triangles. These will serve you and your students well when you begin working with fractional parts and will help you establish the hard-to-learn concept that a whole cannot be made up of more than two halves, four quarters, eight eighths, etc.; and the concept that the larger the numeral of the denominator will be, the smaller the size of the fractional part will be.

Stumbling Blocks

One of the most renowned stumbling blocks for students trying to learn math is problem solving. This is difficult in two ways:

- Reading the words of the problem may be a challenge—even though students may be able to say the words, they may not understand the message;
- The math concepts called for may be what they do not understand—students may not have any idea what processes they ought to try to use in seeking a solution;
- The student may understand the words, choose the correct process, and then do the math wrong and so arrive at the wrong answer.

These are very different difficulties and different techniques will be needed to cure them.

If reading is what is causing the student trouble, begin by reading problems to him or her while they follow the words with their fingers as you read. Discuss the words. Then have the student try again to read it (and help when you sense difficulty). If the math is causing the trouble, discuss the logic in the question and have the student use manipulative materials to work through (with some help from you) what it is that the problem is calling for. If the errors keep occurring in the calculation process, challenge the students to find their errors and review the number facts with them. If it is just carelessness, begin to insist that students recheck their work.

As much time as you need should be spent talking through the logic of problem solving. After all, most of the math we are faced with doing in life situations doesn't appear in the form of algorisms. We have to solve problems.

Another classic stumbling block for students is working with fractions. Much of the difficulty here can be eliminated by spending a good many sessions with real materials. Wholes should be cut in half as many times as necessary to show that there cannot be any more than two halves in a whole, and that there is a difference between two parts and two halves. Go through the same exercises with quarters (fourths), thirds, eighths, sixths, etc.

Once the meaning of fractional parts is thoroughly established, it will be time to deal with manipulating fractions by adding, subtracting, multiplying and dividing them. There are many concepts to deal with here that are not easy to get across. Among them is trying to add fractions with unlike denominators.

If you try to put together a half of a circle and a third of a circle, for example, what will you get? Here you have an opportunity to illustrate the logic behind finding a common denominator and the whole idea of factors. Even more difficult a concept to deal with is how, when multiplying fractions, instead of coming out with a larger quantity (as we do when we multiply whole numbers), we actually end up with a smaller quantity. And harder still to explain is why, when we divide fractions, we end up with a larger quantity.

Too often, teachers merely present the process for getting answers and never deal with the "why" behind the process. This leaves students with a significant gap in understanding even though some of them may learn to come up with a correct answer. The time you take to clarify what is actually happening when fractions are combined will be time very well spent. If you can banish math mysteries, you will be giving your students the opportunity to function well in math for the rest of their lives. Use a good upper-grade math text to simplify the explanations for yourself before presenting them to students.

Adding and subtracting time, and standard weights and measures also present some problems, primarily because these quantities are

not figured on a base-ten system. However, once students really understand "exchange," they ought to have less difficulty with time and
measures.

There are many additional aspects of math tutoring that you should
be aware of and more of them will be taken up in the following chapter.

Chapter 12

BASIC MATH CONCEPTS

A s part of the basics in the tutoring of math, there are a great many concepts which students should understand very thoroughly. You will find some of the more important ones in the list on the pages that follow. Take the time to explain and discuss these basics as you introduce and work with them. Answer the students' questions about anything which causes them to wonder, and be sure to provide enough concrete examples—and challenge your students to provide examples as well—to make the concepts behind each of these subjects absolutely clear. Once you feel sure you have done this, provide time for practice and review. Check on what the students really know and what remains fuzzy.

Resist the temptation to assume students know something because they nod their heads or "look" as though they know. There is the famous story about the math teacher who was working an example on the board and finally saw what she took to be a light of recognition in the eyes of one boy who had not seemed to follow much until that moment. Delighted, she thought she'd check with him. When she asked if he understood or if he had any questions, he admitted that he did have a question. His question was, "Where do all the numbers go when you erase them from the board?" Do not be reluctant to repeat exercises. Your students will, in the long run, appreciate the reinforcement and thrive under it. You will be taking steps to banish the unfathomable muddle with which they have been trying to cope.

Essentials

1. Arithmetic terms —Check to be sure your students know the meanings of at least the following terms:
   - addition, subtraction, multiplication, division;
   - ordinal numbers, cardinal numbers, negative numbers, positive numbers; Arabic numerals; Roman numerals; number line, integer, digit;

- fractions, improper fractions, decimals, mixed numbers;
- commutative principle, distributive principle;
- equations, inequalities, ratio;
- sets, arrays;
- graphs, horizontal axis, vertical axis;
- symmetry, asymmetrical;
- square, rectangle, triangle, circle, cube, sphere, pyramid;
- circumference, area, perimeter, diameter, radius, perpendicular, parallel, tangent;
- plane, dot, line, curve, angle, arch;
- multiples, factors, powers, exponents, square root, cube root;
- theorems, equations, proofs.

2. *Base ten system* — Most of our everyday arithmetic is done in the base ten system. Telling time, standard weights and measures and computer languages are the major notable exceptions. Time depends on base twelve, standard weights and measures depends on memorizing exchange amounts, and computers rely on a base two system. All "base" systems involve establishing place value and using place holders (usually zeros).

- In the base ten system we can use only nine numerals (numbers) plus the zero in any single place (column). It is the place in which a digit sits which lets you know what its value will be.
- A decimal point is the starting point for all number writing, whether or not it actually appears. By accepted practice, we almost never let the decimal point show if it appears at the end of a number, even though it is there and ready to function if it is needed. (25 may be written as 25., or as 25.00, or as 25.00000 without changing its value; no matter how many zeros are added after the decimal point, the number will not change its value unless an integer appears after the zeros.)
- If we start at the decimal point and move to the left one space at a time, we will have columns headed "units," "tens," "hundreds," "thousands," "ten thousands," "hundred thousands," "millions," "ten millions," "hundred millions," "billions," etc.
- If we start at the decimal point and move to the right we will have columns headed "tenths," "hundreths," "thousandths," "ten thousandths," "hundred thousandths," "millionths," etc. An illustration of this appears in Appendix L.

- Students should copy the chart which appears in Appendix K into their arithmetic notebooks.
- They should be given many opportunities to practice reading and writing numbers, both whole numbers and decimal numbers.
- There is in Appendix M a chart which lists the Arabic, Roman, and ordinal numerals.

3. *"Carrying"* — It is much easier to explain the concept of carrying if it is taught as "exchange."
    - Since we cannot fit any number larger than nine (the largest possible single digit number) into a "ones" (unit) column, when we get to the number ten (the first double-digit number), we must exchange our ten ones for one ten.
    - We can see by handling real materials that one "ten" is the same quantity with the same value as ten ones.
    - We represent this quantity as a one in the "tens" column (one ten).
    - And we must put a zero in the ones (unit) column to show that we have no ones left over.
    - Eleven would be one "ten" in the tens column and one "one" in the units column.
    - By extension, the same thing is done when we are exchanging ten tens for one one hundred, ten hundreds for one one thousand, etc. (Use many different kinds of manipulative materials. Actually exchange a bundle of tens for ten ones to explain and vividly illustrate this concept. It will help to fix it in the student's mind.)
    - Not all students will be able to understand the generalization at first. Remember to repeat as often as it takes to be sure the students really do know what happens when we exchange.

4. *Counting* — Counting is either adding, if you are counting up, or it is subtracting, if you are counting down.
    - Counting by ones is adding one more to the previous number.
    - Counting by threes is adding three more to the previous number.
    - Students should practice counting by various numbers.
    - When they first begin to practice, encourage your students to use their fingers to find the next number if they get stuck.
    - The MULTIPLICATION–DIVISION table (See Appendix K)

will be of great help in learning to count by quantities other than one. (Move up and down the columns.)

5. *Division* — Division, especially long division, seems to be the most difficult process for most students to grasp. Part of the reason is the language we use to teach it. Avoid the "goesinta" term entirely (4 "goesinta" 8) and get better results.
   - If we are dividing 45 by 5, we should be asking ourselves how many fives we can find in the quantity 4 (obviously none);
   - Then how many fives we can find in 45;
   - If we know our number facts we know there will be 9 fives in 45;
   - This answer can be checked by referring to the MULTIPLI—CATION–DIVISION table.
   - The process of doing short division (327 divided by 7) should be illustrated with a long division algorism before allowing students to adopt the short division convention.
   - It will more clearly illustrate the "left over" aspect of dividing.
   - It will also show why we do what we do with the leftover number.

Long Division Algorism:

```
         46
    7 | 327
         28x    7 × 4 = 28
         47                 Answer:  46 and 5
         42    7 × 6 = 42            left over
          5
```

Short Division Algorism:

```
            4 6  5/7
      7 |   3 2 7
```

(Be sure to point out that the amount left over after dividing can never be as large as, nor larger than, the divisor.)

6. *Identity elements* — The concept of zero and one as identity elements is important to illustrate.
   - Zero added to or subtracted from a number fails to change the number in any way.
   - "One" multiplied by any number, or any number divided by one, does not change the number.
   - This should be clearly illustrated with manipulative materials.

- The use of the zero as a place holder should also be discussed.

7. *Measurement terms* — Students should learn the values of all of the following:
    - Standard measurement terms, linear, weight and volume (inches, feet, yards, ounces, pounds, quarts, gallons, etc.)
    - Metric measurement terms (millimeters, centimeters, grams, kilograms, liters, etc.).

8. *Numbers and Numerals* — Although the terms are almost always used interchangeably, students should learn that *number* really refers to a quantity and *numeral* refers to the symbol we use to represent that quantity. (Twoness is a quantity and therefore a number; 2 is a symbol standing for that quantity and therefore a numeral.)

9. *Time* — Telling time and calculating time, adding and subtracting hours and minutes (and "exchanging") ought to be practiced until all concepts are clear.

10. *Algorisms* — Be sure to illustrate for your students the various forms arithmetic algorisms can take.

Tutoring Strategies In Mathematics

One of the most important things to remember in tutoring mathematics is that your students have probably poured over an endless number of "examples," sometimes pages of them, in schools or elsewhere as practice. They have gotten some of these right and some of them wrong. Giving these kinds of students sheets of algorisms for practice will very likely prove to be the worst possible turnoff for them. Do not do it. What students who are poor in math need most is constant interaction with someone who understands the difficulties they are having and can accent meaning while appreciating the value of rote for those things which must be memorized (like number facts). Students need to be encouraged with questions and assistance such as:

- How did you get that answer? Show me.
- Why did you do it that way?
- Can you think of another way to do it?
- This is the answer I got. Would you like to try it again?
- Where are you stuck? Show me.
- What is the first step? The next step?

- Use your fingers to figure it out.
- Is that the correct answer to that number fact? Check it on your tables.
- Can you estimate about what your answer might be? How did you do that? Does the answer seem reasonable? (Or—Let's try to do that together.)

Whenever possible, let the burden of correction fall on the students themselves; let them find what may be wrong with what they are doing, but be there to provide direction and help them when you feel help is needed. Try not to say, outright, "That's wrong."

Calculators are universally available these days and students will want to use them. They are wonderful for CHECKING student work but dangerous to rely on for finding answers. Unless a student is fairly proficient at estimating, touching an extra zero or failing to enter a digit when punching in a multi-digit numeral can disastrously distort results. If your students are not proficient at estimating, the answers can be all out of whack. This ought to be illustrated very graphically.

The computer offers access to many excellent programs which software manufacturers sell to help students learn math. Some of them are very effective, but if a machine could have done the work, your student would probably not have come to you for help.

Spend a large portion of your interactive time with students on solving math problems rather than having them work on examples. In math, as we have said throughout these two chapters, it is vital that you help your students develop understanding of what they are doing. If you are tutoring adults, you might wish to devote several sessions to budgeting, tax preparation, credit and interest, discounts, balancing a checkbook and other practical mathematical problems.

Textbooks

There are graded math texts available in every school and in most university and public libraries. Adults will most likely not own math texts and you may or may not want them to buy a book. School students will undoubtedly have their school texts. The books you choose to work from should be used mainly as references and guides, not as straitjackets nor as prescriptions.

Do not make the mistake most teachers make—feeling that you have to cover what the text contains. Even though what a math text covers is of much less importance than what the students are able to grasp as a result of their own trial-and-error work and your guidance, it would probably be extremely difficult—if not impossible—to teach algebra or geometry without a text or at least a workbook.

As a tutor you will find the index of a math text extremely important. There you will have at your fingertips a complete list of what the publisher and author thought to be of major importance in getting the learning across to the student. And by using it you will be able to locate, quickly, all the pages in the text where the subject is taken up.

Whether or not you use a text in your sessions, you should take your cues from the students and build slowly, step by step, from what they really know well to what they can grasp next. Do not just rush ahead trying to expose the student to everything that is in the text. There will always be a tendency to leap ahead, but that is in most cases what was responsible for causing the student to lose out to begin with. Slow and steady, taking nothing for granted, is the way to success with students who have had difficulty learning math.

An excellent book for use in tutoring adults and older children is *Language Development Through Context—Mathematics—Book A—Problem Solving*. A complete citation can be found in the Bibliography.

Chapter 13

TUTORING LANGUAGES

Because of their relative importance as basic knowledge, necessary for normal functioning in our democratic American society, we have devoted several chapters of space to advice on the tutoring of reading and math, almost as though that is where all the opportunity for tutoring exists. Of course, that is not so. There are a great many other opportunities for tutoring, a great many other kinds of things people want to learn as we have already pointed out and, although we are not able to go into the "how's" of all of them in as great detail as we did with reading and math, we will discuss some of them in this and the following chapters.

But the major message which we have already passed on and will continue to stress is that an educator—and that is what a tutor is—must inspire, lead, assist, and guide, but where education is concerned, it is the student who must do the hard work of learning. In no endeavor is this more true than in trying to help foreign speakers to learn how to speak, read and write the English language.

English As A Second (Foreign) Language—ESL

Our public schools across the country do a commendable job of teaching school-age children who were raised speaking languages other than ours how to speak, read and write in English. But there are fewer resources available, outside of the large cities, where the non-English-speaking parents of these newcomers, as well as other non-English-speaking adults, can go for help in learning the English language and American customs.

For a while, teaching English to foreign-speaking people was a service not very much in demand. Now it is being sought after in much the same way it had been in the big cities in the early years of the twentieth century.

Today, many Japanese, Central and South Americans, Europeans, Africans, Chinese and other Asians are coming here, some to settle,

109

others sent by their companies, not to settle, but to spend several years working in offices and factories before returning home. Although some of these folks arrive knowing how to speak some English, many more do not. Even those who do speak the language often know little about how to function easily in our culture.

Even though one may consider it surprising, it has been shown to be true, over and over again, that it is not really necessary to know how to say any words in a person's native language in order to be able to help him or her learn your language. For us, we only need to feel comfortable with our knowledge of English to be able to help others learn it.

If you are going to tutor English, your initial lessons will have to center around some innovative communicating. You will find that you are using a combination of acting out, creating, illustrating, singing, humming, props and body movements, limited only by the extent of your imagination and your need to find ways to get messages to and from your non-English-speaking clients.

However, before you have even a first session with a foreign client, it is a very good idea for you to try to learn something about his or her culture. Different cultures have different taboos and ascribe different meanings to what we might consider ordinary behavior:

- For some it is quite rude to touch anyone unless you are very intimate.
- For some it is rude to look a person in the eye (especially a teacher, who is considered someone of high status). Averted eyes are a sign of respect.
- For some, the response to "Do you understand?" will always have to be yes even if they haven't a clue about what you are trying to get across. It would be rude to say no.

Knowing at the outset about mores like this will be bound to make things easier for you as you begin to work with foreign students and may keep you from making potentially embarrassing mistakes.

There are places where you can obtain information concerning cultural differences:

- The Center For Applied Linguistics, P.O. Box 37422, Washington, D.C. 20013
- United States Department of Education Refugee Materials Center, 324 East 11 Street, 9th Floor, Kansas City, Missouri, 64106

You can also consult an encyclopedia for some kinds of information about the country your student has come from, its geography, agriculture, government, and ethnicity. National Geographic Society can also be very helpful in providing you with information.

First Steps—Finding Clients

Of course your very first steps if what you want to do is tutor English as a second (foreign) language will have to be centered on finding clients— making contact with those who need your service. This will not be very easy, since you will not be able to communicate directly with your prospective clients in their language. Still, there are several things you can do at the beginning to contact potential clients:

- Contact the personnel officer in any local factories or businesses known to be employing foreign-speaking people and leave copies of your business card, your tutoring resume, and, in addition, a simple flyer (described below).
- With the help of some of the local clergy and the head of the community school in your area, identify some local people who speak the foreign languages you are targeting and who also speak English.
- Get help from them in designing a simple multi-lingual advertisement (flyer) stating the fact that you are prepared to tutor foreign-speaking people in American-English. (See Appendix N for an example of such an advertisement.)
- Place an ad in local newspapers, penny-savers, and community and religious newsletters and send it to personnel officers as indicated above.
- Inform your network of contacts in the community that you are now going to be teaching English as a foreign language.

Be sure to prepare yourself for your first meeting with any prospective clients who contact you. If at all possible, have a translator present at that first contact session. The translator may be an adult or a child, as long as he or she can assist in allowing simple messages to pass between you and your non-English-speaking prospective client.

Think about the essential messages you want to get across at that initial meeting. The information you will want from your client will include the responses to as many of the following inquiries as possible. The more you learn, the better you will be able to plan your tutoring sessions, which will obviously be different if you are working with someone who is highly educated and perhaps knows a little English from what they would be if your student is illiterate in his or her own language and knows no English at all. Ask about:

1. Your client's name (get it as it sounds if he or she cannot write it).
2. Your client's address and telephone number.
3. Your client's native language and whether it uses the same alphabet we do.
4. Whether your client can read and write in his or her native language.
5. The educational level your client achieved in the other country and in the USA, if any.
6. The job, or the kind of work your client did in the other country and in the USA if any.
7. The composition of your client's family. (Your client may or may not want to give you these answers. Be sensitive to a potential need for privacy.)
   - How many members are there in the family?
   - Is there a spouse?
   - Are there sons? How many?
   - Are there daughters? How many?
   - Are there parents? How many?
   - Which of the family members are in the USA?
   - Where are the others?
8. What other languages does your client know besides the native language?

The information you want your client to receive from you concerning the tutoring you are offering should be prepared in advance, ready for him or her to take home. Such information should include:

- An index card with your name and your per-session fee written on it.
- A calendar which you will review during the session and which clearly illustrates the day and time of the sessions you will be offering and the length of each session. (You may wish to wait and establish this with the client during the first actual tutoring session.)
- A copy of your attendance policy.

- A copy of your tutoring resume and your business card with your telephone number clearly underlined.
- An illustrated list of what you would like your client to bring to the next tutoring session (notebook, pencil, etc.).

Methods

Hearing words in a language that is unfamiliar to you, and understanding those words well enough to act on them, is much more difficult than speaking those words. People new to a language can often say what they want to say but cannot make out the meaning of the native speaker's response. One of your tasks in tutoring is going to be to help your students learn to hear and understand not only what you say but also what other American speakers, who will be much less careful in their speech than you, are saying.

The way to begin to do this is with simple everyday sentences. Say them slowly but with the correct intonation. Don't shout. Talking louder than normally necessary will in no way make it easier for your students to understand you. They are not, after all, hard of hearing. Act out or in some way illustrate, preferably with concrete objects, what you are trying to get across.

Sentences Useful In Teaching ESL

The following sentences are suggestive and will serve as the basis for many lessons. If the student knows no English, you will probably have to use a variety of techniques to get across the meaning of even the simplest sentences. Write, draw, use pictures, gesture, repeat. Help students provide you with answers. As students learn to say and use new words, write them on cards. The student may or may not wish to put his or her translation on the back of those cards. In an early lesson, be sure to teach the student the following sentences:

- I don't understand.
- Please say that another way.
- Please say that more slowly.
- Thank you.
- Hello.
- Good-bye.

- Please help me.

In an introductory session you may also wish to use some of the following:

Hello.
My name is. . . . What is your name?
Can you spell your name? Please spell (write) your name.
Where do you live? What is your address? Please write it.
Do you have a telephone? What is your number?
Where are you from? What country? What city?
Did you go to school in your country? For how long?
Do you read and write in your language?
How did you get here? Why are you here?
What work did you do in your country?
What work will you do here?
How many people are there in your family? What is the name of
   your . . . (husband, wife, son(s) daughter(s))?
How old are your children? Please write their names.

In later sessions you might want to use some or all of the following:

Emergencies

Dial 911. Say:

"We need help at (address). We do not speak English. We need (police, ambulance, etc.)"

Money

Use actual coins and bills and checks and bank deposit and withdrawal slips:

Show me a . . . (nickel, penny, dime, quarter, half-dollar)
How much is this?
Where is the . . . ?
Please give me. . . .
What does that cost?
SALE. What does that mean?
This costs $2.98. Please give me change from $5.00.
This check is like money. (Explain)
This is how a deposit (withdrawal) slip works.
Read this number: Thirty-five dollars and fifteen cents.
Read this number: $47.50. Show me how much that is.

Time

This is a clock (watch). It is now five after ten. It is a quarter to three. We have lunch at noon. It is dark at midnight. It is half-past twelve. It is a quarter after one. This is how we write eight twenty-seven — 8:27. What time is it? How late is it?

Calendar

This is a calendar. The names of the months are. . . . Show me February. The names of the days are. Show me Thursday. Show me the first Tuesday in May. These are important American holidays. Find Christmas. Find your birthday. What is today? What is today's date?

Directions

This is the top (bottom). My hand is going up (down). My hand is rising (falling). The rain is falling. The book is on (off) the table. The pencil is under (over) the book. This is my right (left) hand. The map shows the directions and they are north, east, south, west. The store is straight ahead. His house is back there. Turn down that street. Stop at the red light. Go when the light turns green. Come here.

Colors, Shapes, Sizes

What are the names of the primary colors? What color is this? Show me a red crayon. Point to a square (triangle, rectangle, sphere, circle). The big red ball is a round sphere. This box is big and this is bigger. That one is small and the one over there is smaller. He is tall. He is short.

Over-the-Counter Medicines

We use aspirin (Tylenol, Nuperin, etc.) for headaches. We use the following antacids. We use Band-Aid strips for cuts. We use antiseptics (name several) for cleaning wounds. These are brand names of tooth-pastes, mouthwashes, soaps, sanitary pads, cotton swabs, shaving creams, deodorants, condoms, etc.

Household

The names of the rooms in the house are. . . . The names of the pieces of furniture in the living room are. . . . The names of the fixtures in the kitchen (bathroom) are. . . . This is a wall (window, door, lock, floor, carpet, ceiling, light, lamp). These are the stairs (steps). We use a hose to water the garden.

Clothing and Body Parts

On our feet we wear . . . (stockings, socks, slippers, shoes, boots, sneakers). On our legs we wear . . . (pants, panty hose, shorts, jeans, slacks). On our bodies we wear . . . (underwear, panties, boxer shorts, briefs, bras, slips, undershirts, tee shirts). Over our underwear we wear . . . (shirts, ties, blouses, jackets, sweaters, suits, dresses). On our heads we wear . . . (hats, caps, scarfs, kerchiefs). On our hands we wear gloves or mittens. The parts of my body are: face, hair, brow, forehead, eyebrows, eyes, cheeks, mouth, lips, teeth, tongue, ears, earlobes, chin, neck, etc.

Ordinary Commands, Greetings, Etc.:

Sit. Sit down. Stand. Stand up. Get up. Move. Move over. Get out. Get out of the way. Go away. Come here. Let's go. Hi. So long. Bye-bye. See you later.

Foods

For breakfast we might have . . . (cereal, eggs, juice, toast, bread, coffee, tea, milk, cocoa, fruit). For lunch we may have . . . (sandwich, soda, soup, salad, pasta). For dinner we may have . . . (meat, fish, chicken, turkey, pork, rice, vegetables, soup).
Some common cereals are . . . (oatmeal, corn flakes, bran flakes, rice puffs or crispies, etc.)
Some common juices are . . . (tomato, orange, cranberry, apple, pineapple, grapefruit).
Some common vegetables are . . . (green beans, lima beans, peas, potatoes, lettuce, tomatoes, carrots, radishes, green peppers, squash, sprouts, yams, etc.)

All of the following will also be helpful things to do, but DO NOT TRY TO DO THEM ALL IN ONE LESSON.

- Have your students repeat each sentence after you say it. Then you say it again.
- Break the sentence down into individual words and then recombine them. Have the students repeat each word.
- Write the sentences if your student can read.
- Provide your students with hand-held mirrors. Have them watch your mouth as you say each sentence, each word, each recombined sentence. Then have them watch their own mouths as they repeat what you have just said.
- Have them note the rise and fall of your voice by raising and lowering their hands as you speak a declarative sentence, a question, an exclamation.
- Have your students copy into their notebooks the simple sentences you are practicing (if they can write).

NOTE: You will find, listed in the Bibliography, a book called *PD'S In-Depth Pronunciation Aural Discrimination Drills for Learners of English.* Try to obtain a copy. It will be quite helpful to you.

People new to the country often do not understand our ways and do not know some of the simple day-to-day skills we take for granted, like how to shop in a supermarket. During every lesson you should include instruction in some of the survival skills people might need in order to function (cope) successfully. People who are expert at teaching English to the foreign born have developed the following list of these important skills.

Survival Skills In America

The following skills are important for the newcomer to acquire as quickly as possible. These are minimums. Many additional skills can be added to this list.

- Ability to recognize warning signs (danger, poison).
- Ability to both speak and hear simple sentences with understanding.
- Ability to use the telephone and a phone book.
- Ability to handle money with understanding.
- Ability to market for the family in supermarkets.
- Ability to purchase clothing and other necessities.
- Ability to obtain a driver's license.
- Ability to function in a banking relationship (mortgages, credit cards).
- Ability to use a checkbook and keep balances.
- Ability to ask for directions and understand the responses.
- Ability to read and understand a map.
- Ability to communicate with real-estate people.
- Ability to register children in schools and provide the schools with necessary information.
- Ability to seek employment.
- Ability to locate appropriate health care personnel.

Useful Words To Know For Filling Out Forms

date	citizen	education
month	citizenship status	years of schooling
year	birth date	last school attended
name	date of birth	degrees held
Mr.	place of birth	diplomas held
Mrs.	age	salary
Miss	height	hourly
first name	weight	weekly
last name	Social Security number	part-time
maiden name	marital status	full-time
middle name	married	temporary work
middle initial	separated	sex
address	divorced	male
street	widowed	female
permanent address	single	health plan coverage
mailing address	occupation	medical history
present address	employer	previous conditions
zip code	firm	physical impairment
city	place of employment	driver's license
state	self-employed	number
telephone number	length of service	signature
business telephone	references	
home telephone	in case of emergency	

You might wish to rent from a library (or buy) some practice tapes with exercises on speaking English. Or you may want to make up and tape such exercises yourself. If so, the following are some suggestions:

- Using a tape recorder, say a sentence slowly.
- Say, "Repeat the sentence, please."
- Pause long enough to say it again at the same rate in your head.
- Say the next sentence.
- Use the "repeat" command.
- Permit your students to borrow the tapes for practice at home.
- Be sure to devote the largest part of every lesson to interactive speaking between you and your student.

Review the section on teaching the alphabet in Chapter 9 on "Reading." Learning how to read and sound out the English alphabet will be very important to all those who are foreign speaking, but especially to those who are not familiar with the configuration or the sounds of our letters.

In an early lesson, teach your students to sign their name using our alphabet. Teach them how to read and write your name also.

Vocabulary development is very important. The easiest way to begin learning words is with nouns which can be shown as real objects or as pictures. Shortly you will find that you can move to combining the nouns with simple action verbs. Picture books, magazines, children's toys, pencil and paper, and anything you can find that can be labeled will, in your early days with the student, be valuable as learning aids.

- Point to the pictures; say the words; label whatever in the picture can be labeled; have the student say the words.
- Post labels on any objects in the room that can be named this way; have the student read the label.
- Encourage students to label objects in their own homes and to practice naming them.
- Teach the names for the parts of the body. (Head, eyes, nose, mouth, teeth, tongue, etc.)
- Teach the pronunciation and the written names of the numbers. Go as high as your student seems able.
- Teach the days of the week and the months of the year.
- Teach the clock and the way we tell time.
- Conjugate simple action verbs with antecedent pronouns and teach all of the pronouns.
- Help your students to hear the likely responses to the simple sentences they are learning to say. Much repetition is likely to be necessary before they will be able to do this. Stress the fact that you know this is hard to do. Do not allow them to be discouraged.
- Introduce adjectives and adverbs with illustrations and by acting out the concepts (hot, very hot; cold, very cold; ugly, very ugly; etc.)
- Introduce the concept of "not."
- Introduce "articles" (the, a, an) and all the other parts of speech as you use them in your conversations with your students.
- Be sure to write the words you are using whenever you think that by doing so you will clarify what you are saying.
- Be sure to check for understanding many times during each session. This is especially important since you are not relying on translation at all.
- Don't try to cover too much at any one session. Remember that repetition and practice are vital.
- Provide opportunities for acting things out along with speaking and listening.

- Have your students write sentences from your dictation and then help them write simple sentences of their own.
- Review and carefully correct all of their written work.
- Have students rewrite each exercise correctly.

NOTE: In Appendix I, there is a functional reading word list for adults which you will probably find very helpful.

You might wish to have your students memorize and discuss the meaning of several nursery rhymes and children's poems. These are rhythmic, easy to learn and help increase vocabulary.

- Be sensitive to the fact that your students may feel insulted by being asked to learn children's verses.
- Stress that they are useful for training the ear and that they can use the rhymes for entertaining their own children.
- You may be interested in bringing in some simple children's books. The same messages should be given with regard to these.

You would be well advised to make liberal use of the tape recorder to tape both yourself and your students.

- As your students become more familiar with English, have them read stories onto tape, one paragraph at a time, and intersperse their reading with your own rendition of the same selections.
- Encourage your students to take home the tapes you make together and listen to them at home.
- Encourage your students to watch some educational TV programs to get the feel of the language.

Introduce the idiomatic expressions your clients are likely to need as soon as you think they will be able to grasp their meaning. Two- or three-word phrases which we take for granted can cause problems—especially since their meanings cannot be found in the dictionary—for example:

- get up (rise; stand)
- get down (descend; kneel; squat)
- dig in (eat; begin; resist)
- watch out (be careful)
- simmer down (control your excitement)
- beat it (leave now; leave quickly)
- knock it off (stop what you are doing)
- butt out (do not interfere)

- hang up, hang out, hang around, hang on, etc.

Teach your students to ask people to "Please say that a different way," when they do not understand.

Newspaper headlines, are a great primary source for idioms and slang.

- Bears Murder Tigers At Home (The Chicago team won.)
- Giants Kill Reds (The New York team beat the Cincinnati team in baseball.)
- Mayor Faces Down Right Wing (The mayor wins in a face-to-face confrontation with conservatives)

An interesting concept that you will, at some point, have to share with your students is that the many different accents which English-speaking people use are likely to make words sound different, depending on who is speaking them. Indeed, there is a book called *How To Speak Southern* which has listed (among many others) words such as:

- Airs (errors, mistakes)—She made three "airs".
- Ah (I)—"Ah" don't think "ah" like it.
- Awl (oil)—The car needs "awl."
- Far (fire)—There's a "far" in the "farplace."

Once again, it has to be stressed that your support is vital as your students work to make their way through the muddle of sounds that regional accents tack on to standard speaking patterns.

Be sure to remember the basic theme of this book as you work with your students:

IT'S NOT WHAT YOU TEACH OR HOW YOU TEACH IT THAT IS IMPORTANT. WHAT IS IMPORTANT IS WHAT AND HOW YOUR STUDENTS LEARN.

That is a simple message, but if you keep it in mind you will always be placing the emphasis on the correct things as you work with your clients.

There will probably be a bonus for you in working with non-English-speaking people. By the time they are able to speak English with a degree of competency and understanding, you will probably have learned a great many of the words and expressions of their language, too.

And remember that the basic lesson for teaching English as a foreign language is: REPEAT—REPEAT—REPEAT.

Chapter 14

TUTORING IN OTHER AREAS

Although we've talked about tutoring reading, math, and English as a second language, we've hardly scratched the surface of the market. There are an almost unlimited number of opportunities for a person with the desire to help people learn. We will discuss some of them in this chapter and more of them in the next, but, remember, it just isn't possible to cover all of the possibilities which exist.

Your own alertness is what will serve you best when you decide to enter the business of tutoring for pay. Look, listen and be ready to step in when you learn about a need that someone has to improve or increase his or her knowledge or ability in some field. If you can help, you have a beckoning tutoring opportunity.

Tutoring A Foreign Language

Most of the methods suggested in the previous chapter on tutoring English as a foreign language apply as well to the tutoring of a foreign language to English-speaking students. However, when you are tutoring English speakers, you as a tutor have important additional advantages. The biggest advantage is that you speak and understand both languages so you will be able, more easily, to translate, to move back and forth from one language to the other. You will also be able to help your students translate.

On the other hand, if it is possible for people to learn English by using what little they know of it as the only available means of communication from the outset, it is also possible for the English speaking to learn another language in the very same way, especially if their primary purpose is to be able to communicate quickly, rather than to become scholars in the language. What is more, research has shown that when you are forced to learn a language by conversing in it, you learn it faster and better and it tends to remain with you longer, especially if you have the opportunity to use it from time to time.

We therefore suggest that to the extent possible, you help your students learn a foreign language by using the same basic approaches suggested in the previous section, adding lessons in translating only when that becomes appropriate. Develop lists of necessary words which parallel those in Chapter 13. Construct a list of survival skills for anyone visiting the country or countries where the native language is the one you are teaching. Plan several lessons around the culture and mores of the people, the food they eat and the clothing they wear.

There will, of course, be a place in your tutoring program for conjugating verbs, learning the correct grammar and spelling, and reading and writing in the new language, but those more formal things can come after early lessons in basic conversation and communication. This approach follows the one we all use in our native languages. We learn to speak (communicate) first, focusing on those words which are most likely to get us what we want. We learn the formal aspects of the language later.

Even if your students have come to you because they are doing poorly in their language studies in school, you can begin with conversational lessons. It will take a little longer to get to the work they are faced with in school, but then, by the time they do get there, your students will have developed an ease and a familiarity with the sounds and structure of the language, and then the grammar, spelling and vocabulary development will be less of a chore.

As you move into concentration on the more formal aspects of the language, you may want to use a text. If your clients are students attending school, they may have one. If not, there are a variety of texts available in college bookstores and in commercial bookstores. The main values of texts are their organization and the exercises they provide. Most texts present information in a series of logical sequences, usually moving from the simple to the more complex, with a variety of practice exercises after each presentation. This can be either helpful or stifling, depending on how closely one adheres to what the text is presenting.

If you plan to use a text, plan to move about in it in ways that will keep your students interested. There is, however, nothing to say that you have to use a textbook. If your students are with you to learn to read and write in the language, bookstores have both modern and classic literature from which you can work, skipping the text entirely should you wish to do so.

One of the least interesting ways to learn a language is to be given lists of vocabulary words to memorize. On the other hand, concentrating on realistic sentences, idiomatic expressions, rhymes, songs, simple stories, practical skills and correct pronunciations of words usually captures and sustains the interest of students. Just as, when we were tutoring English to foreign speakers, we made labels for everything in the environment which was able to hold a label, you should encourage your students to do the same. Have them tag all of the furniture at home, everything in the kitchen and bathroom, articles of their clothing, even food.

Buy a child's coloring book with pictures of the city, the country, the farm, the airport, the highway, etc. Have your students label each item in the pictures. In later lessons they can write sentences (and soon even paragraphs) telling about the action occurring in the pictures.

Take every possible opportunity to have your students speak. Have them repeat words and sentences after you. Have them listen to native speakers on recorded tapes. Have them use mirrors to watch their mouths as they speak. Make tapes of them as they speak and read. Keep them actively involved in every lesson.

Remember, it is what the student is able to learn that matters, not what or how much you teach. And once again, just as in tutoring English as a second language—REPEAT—REPEAT—REPEAT.

Computers As A New Tutoring Market

Computers are everywhere today. They ring up the prices of our food at the supermarket, keep track of our accounts at the bank and our bills on our credit cards. They are in our children's classrooms, in almost every office and factory, in the libraries and museums. They even control some of the functions in our cars and many in our airplanes.

Unfortunately, most people, who have never interacted directly with a computer of their own, regard them with suspicion. They believe that computers are so complex that they will never be able to learn how to use them. Some even tend to believe that all computers are something like "HAL," or the one Spock uses on the *Enterprise* —that you just ask a question and in some unfathomable way the computer makes the whole of human history immediately available. Of course, these are misconceptions. Today's computers can do a great deal, but they can't do that much. They are specialists ready to "output" combinations of what someone has "input" and permitting a user to access stored information in a variety of ways, depending on the particular software program the user is working with.

The wonderful thing is that there is a huge and growing market for the services of people who know how to provide the input needed by the computer, who know how to write the programs which allow the user to access the input, and who know how to fix what may go wrong with a computer. There are people everywhere who want to learn how to do all these things.

There was a time, and it was only a few years ago, when only businesses with a great deal of money and a whole lot of space could afford to own a computer. Today, that is no longer true. Computers continue to grow smaller, more powerful, and less expensive. PC's (personal computers) are found in more and more homes. They are often bought for the children and the adults in the house carefully tiptoe around them, afraid to touch them for fear of messing up something.

Because of this combination of suspicion and fear, too many of these very powerful machines do nothing but play games when they could be used to provide us with information on anything we are curious about and make many things in our lives easier.

Anyone can learn to use a computer. If you are one of those who uses one now and you wish to provide instruction in this field (and you can, even if you are not a "hacker"), that is a vital message for you to get across to potential clients. And the place to begin to spread your message is in your advertisements seeking clients.

What can you offer to the army of people who are still certain that computer use is far too complex a challenge for them? You might start with a short series of sessions devoted to introducing the computer, in which you present the most often used terms (input, output, RAM, ROM, K, modem, mouse, ASCI, Fortran, Basic, software, hardware, disk, keyboard, monitor, terminal, printer, surge suppressor, etc.). During these sessions you can explain how a computer works, the design of disks and diskettes, and perhaps even explain the "base-two" system (see Appendix L).

You might want to illustrate how we use certain code words to access the memory stored in either the hardware or the software, and, by using them, we instruct the computer to perform calculations or recombinations of one sort or another; then we are able to call forth output in the new or recombined form by using another set of code words.

As applies to tutoring in any field, you would want to get your students involved in "hands-on" exercises as quickly and as frequently as possible. Once they begin to use a simple program and interact with a keyboard, a monitor and a printer, excitement is bound to replace anxiety.

When working with a computer, even on a simple exercise, becomes possible, much of the mystery is taken away and when the mystery goes, the fear goes, too.

Most people who have interacted with computers have had experiences with both hardware and software which brought them to a standstill. "Bugs" and "glitches" can be frustrating. One of the services you can provide, even to longtime users, is help in interpreting the manuals which come with programs. If you are able to read a manual and then follow its instructions so that you cure computer glitches, if you can teach others how to provide that kind of troubleshooting service even to their own machines, you will be much in demand as a tutor. A great course to offer would be, "How To Be A Hacker."

You might want to provide sessions devoted to creating "programs." Many users would like to know how to design their own software so that it is tailored to do exactly the jobs they want done. Once they know Basic, or Fortran, or DBase, or any one of a number of other computer languages, they will be able to create their own programs and be much less limited in what they can have their computers do for them.

Additional suggestions for what you as a Computer tutor might offer could include:

- Graphic Design and Computer Art
- Programs for Parents and Children
- Word processing
- Spread sheeting
- Using Available Educational Software
- Desktop Publishing
- Creative Computer Use for Earning Money
- Computers for the Pre-School Set
- Modems and Using Commercial Data Bases
- Playing Computer Games

As you can see, the opportunities are there. Of course, what you can offer depends on how much you, yourself, can do with the hardware and software you have available. The potential for setting up either one-to-one or small group sessions is limited only by your access to a computer, your knowledge of hardware and software, and your ability to reach the public and let them know about the instruction and information you can make available to them.

How you advertise will determine the number of clients who seek your assistance. (See Appendix O for suggested advertising copy.) After that, it will be the quality of your instruction and your interaction with your students that will determine your continued success.

Home Crafts (Sewing, Cooking, Needlework, Gardening, Etc.)

Most people don't think about the homemaking skills they have acquired as something they might use to earn some money, but there are many folks out there who would love to learn how to knit, crochet, make a dress or some drapes, arrange flowers artistically, or even fix a gourmet meal. What is most important if you are hoping to do some tutoring in one of these areas (and we always come back to it) is to advertise your service in such a way that it is instantly attractive. Your advertisement should spell out clearly exactly what it is that you are proposing to help someone learn and why they should want to learn it.

To run such classes (and these skills are usually better taught in classes than individually because your students will enjoy and learn from their interaction with each other), you have to appeal to people enough to make them want to leave home to learn what you have to offer them. (See suggestions for advertising in Appendix N.)

Once you have your client group, it is vital that you establish a workshop atmosphere by getting each person started on making something at the very first session. A sense of accomplishment is what will keep your clients coming back session after session.

Encourage your students to take notes on the information they pick up during the sessions. Provide them with handouts from time to time, but ask them to copy what they'd like to keep from those papers and then return them to you at the next session. (Do not neglect to collect them.) This accomplishes several things:

- People learn as they write because writing focuses concentration on content.
- No class time will be spent on taking notes.
- There will be some work done by students between sessions.
- Your students will value the notes more if they have spent time copying them.
- You will have your handouts to use again with future students.

Remember to keep individual student records and keep current with what each of your students is involved in producing. Plan to move each one along, finishing one project and beginning another, accomplishing something new at each session. If your students are working on projects that they can finish at home, by all means encourage them to do so. Be sure to arrange for viewing space for finished projects. You might even want to sponsor a periodic "show" for the products your students have completed.

Remember that besides coming to learn a new skill, your clients are coming to sessions like these to have a good time. Make each session as pleasant as possible for each person attending. Do not spend all of your time with those who are most skillful, but don't ignore them either. Just because they are capable does not mean they do not need your assistance and encouragement.

Shopwork Crafts

Tutoring in areas in which a workshop is needed such as such as woodworking, sculpture, ceramics, carpentry, home repair, plumbing, electricity, electronics, or auto mechanics is similar to tutoring the homemaking crafts. The major difference is that you will undoubtedly need a more extensive workshop or studio and a more extensive collection of tools to do this work. It is for that reason that many who look to teach in these areas seek positions in high schools, trade schools or community schools where well-stocked workshops are available to them and their potential students.

Of course, there is nothing to say that you can't use your home as a workshop. In fact, there may be situations in which you go to a client's home to provide on-the-spot tutoring such as assistance in home repair projects or reconstruction of a piece of furniture. The same suggestions as those made in the previous "Home Crafts" section apply to your interaction with your students in these shop areas. It would be a good idea to reread them.

Students should be busily engaged in hands-on work from the very first session on and, if possible, they should work out a plan of activities which will have them involved in a series of projects over an agreed upon time period. Don't forget before beginning shopwork classes to pay attention to the admonition to devote a block of time to the rules for safety in the workshop and to review these rules with your students periodically. And don't forget that your students will be proud of what they produce. If it is possible, arrange to have their finished products displayed where they can be viewed by other students as well as outsiders.

Games And Leisure-time Activities

Tutoring in this area can be more fun than hard work. On the other hand, you are not going to be doing the playing. You are going to be helping others to play and that can often turn out to be frustrating.

There is a tendency when giving instruction in game playing to recite a bevy of rules for your students to learn. We have found that a more interesting approach is to get right into the game itself. A simple statement is enough to begin with:

THE OBJECT OF THIS GAME IS...

Every game has an objective. If students know what that is from the outset, it will help them to focus their attention on your presentations and to concentrate on what they must do to learn how to play.

The playing of every game requires some skill, some luck, and some knowledge of the rules. The rules can be listed, copied and memorized. They can also be given to the student in printed form. Students are more likely to learn rules, to learn them better, and to learn them faster if they have copied them—a few at a time—and had them explained and illustrated with concrete examples when they were copying them. This is especially true of complex games such as bridge.

Luck is something none of us can control, but as a games tutor you can help your students to recognize what luck they have and how to make the most of it. This can often be the difference between winning and losing. Developing skill in playing games is very much like developing skill at anything else we do—it is a matter of continuing practice. This is something students must do for themselves. The only help you can offer in this respect is providing opportunity and perhaps a location for such practice.

One of the best places to find clients and even whole classes in need of tutors for games and other leisure time activities is through the Parks and Recreation Department of your town. Sometimes they will even take the responsibility of organizing classes for you. Community schools on all levels are additional sources of clients. Again, don't discount the power of advertising. Even in offering instruction in how to play, the way you let people know about you is all important.

Chapter 15

ADDITIONAL OPPORTUNITIES FOR TUTORING

As we have said before, we have only begun to scratch the surface as far as opportunities for tutoring are concerned. In this chapter we will be discussing some more of these fields, but we will not be covering such areas as teaching the signing language of the deaf, teaching animal obedience, teaching film development or camera use, or many, many other things. If you plan to do any tutoring in these fields, what we have suggested as methods in other areas will certainly be—to a very large extent—applicable. It should not take much to adapt the recommendations made in this chapter and in the chapters that preceded this one to your specific enterprise. Take what you know and share it with others.

Tutoring In The Arts

Talented people have been providing instruction in the studio arts throughout human history. All such instruction seems to combine three important approaches:

- Demonstration—which shows the student what can be done and gives him or her something for which to strive;
- Analysis (including critique)—which helps the student to think through the processes involved in creating the art;
- Trial and error—which allows the student to attempt to perform even though at first the performance may be anything but artistic, to fail, and to continue to try.

The demonstration and analysis are largely what the tutor is expected to provide. The trial and error is the domain of the learner and it must be followed by practice to eliminate what does not work and perfect what does. Unless the learner has an extraordinary gift, early attempts on his or her part are likely to be clumsy and lacking in inspiration, vision and skill. The role of the tutor, especially in the early stages, is to guide, to mentor and to encourage.

It takes hard work to train fingers to hit the correct notes in the correct rhythmic patterns so that music results when piano keys are depressed. It takes more than a brush filled with paint splashing across a newly stretched canvass to create a sensitive artistic picture. It takes more than a mallet and a chisel to create a sculpture with the power to impress. It takes more than a dictionary and a word processor to create a good novel. It takes more than merely learning lines of a play to present a believable moving performance. And it takes more than a swaying body and two prancing feet to create a dance.

On the other hand, producing an artistic creation is not merely a matter of inspiration. Artists must learn the how's and why's of their craft well enough to be able to translate their inspiration into aesthetic production. That is where you, the tutor, have a role to play. You must be able to advise students:

- On which tools and materials to purchase;
- On which books to read;
- On which music to listen to and which sheet music to purchase;
- On which concerts, dramas and dance recitals to attend;
- On which galleries to visit.

You will be the one who will guide them concerning which postures, strokes, movements, colors, intonations, structures, and plots do "work" and which do not. And, of course, you are the one who will be able to arrange for your students to display their talents to fellow students and others by setting up art shows, music or dance recitals, readings, and dramatic productions.

Producing art is hard work and honing artistic skills generally takes so much practice and single-mindedness that students tend to fall away from instruction after a while. This is something you ought to be prepared for. Don't be discouraged by it. Most of your students are not taking lessons in the art you are teaching in order to become professionals in the field.

Students usually come to art for their own pleasure. They do not really expect to produce the greatest novel ever written, nor to be invited to perform in a Broadway play. You as a tutor, are helping them to develop a skill they can pick up on again whenever they feel they'd like to do so. Your work with them helps them develop an ability which will enrich their existence for the rest of their lives. It is truly a gift to them, even if they only practice for their own pleasure.

Exercise And Athletics

All over the country these days there are people going into the business of providing aerobics classes for those who wish to exercise. There are instructors working in salons devoted entirely to exercise. People are leading exercise classes in swimming pools. Coaches and coaching assistants are working with amateur sports teams, semi-professional teams and professional teams. Schools are using trainers, both as volunteers and as part of the paid staff.

If you are planning to tutor in any of the physical training or athletics fields, be certain to check what the health laws are in the community in which you plan to work. There are some activities for which you will have to be licensed and have special training before you are permitted to conduct classes. There are others for which no special licenses will be needed.

Body wrapping, tanning, dieting, weight-loss programs and toning activities all attract their share of consumers these days. All of these activities provide leadership or tutoring opportunities for those interested in body conditioning and improvement.

Before taking forays into any of these fields, it would be wise to consult with local experts—people who are already working in the field—about what the requirements might be and what special training you ought to seek that you may not already have. It might also be a good idea to begin by working for someone else for awhile to get the feel of the market before opening your own service.

Tutoring For The Development Of Study Skills

Too many students who are failing to succeed in school have just never learned how to study. They have never learned how to:

- Scan a page for information
- Pick out key words and phrases
- Outline
- Take notes
- Develop mnemonic devices
- Concentrate
- Become interested in studying anything.

There are suggestions throughout this book for how to help students master some of these skills. In addition, there are a few specific tutoring suggestions which apply directly to study skill development. These include:

1. Scanning a page for information: (Be sure to discuss the purpose of scanning and point out the difference in purpose between scanning—to pick up the gist of a passage quickly—and reading—to obtain all the information provided in a passage.)
   - To scan successfully, a student needs to develop confidence in his or her reading ability and trust in the fact that the eye can take in information very quickly.
   - Have students practice moving their eyes quickly, sweeping over a paragraph; then cover the paragraph and ask that they try to tell you what the central message conveyed was.
   - After several such practice sessions students ought to be less resistant and more adept at scanning.
2. Picking out key words and phrases: Have students scan for these using questions asking for limited kinds of information, such as:
   - "Where does it say . . . ?"
   - "What was the color of her coat?"
   - "How many people were there?"
3. Outlining: Discuss the reasons for outlining.
   - The need to note the most important information in an article, a chapter, a book, etc.
   - The need to organize one's own thoughts.
4. Outlining: Present the key elements used in outlining and provide opportunities for practicing them, including:
   - Using a notation system of either letters or numbers.
   - Using indentations when subtopics are noted.
   - Stressing the need for consistency.
5. Taking notes:
   - Listening for what is most important.
   - Using correct outline format.
   - Jotting key words and phrases rather than sentences.
6. Developing mnemonic devices: Help students develop the skill of creating memory stimulators.
7. Concentrating:
   - Provide drills in blocking out everything but a given topic for a minute. (Eyes closed, ears covered.)

- Increase the time by ten seconds at a time.
- Do not do more than one or two of these exercises in any session.
- Urge the student to practice this at home with a cooking timer, gradually (by ten-second intervals) increasing the concentrating time.

Test-Taking Skills

There are all kinds of additional study skills you can offer to students, including the skill of how to take an objective test. Many don't even know how to budget their time, how to move from the questions to the appropriate place on the answer sheets, how to find key words, or how to handle their nervousness. You can help students prepare to be successful test takers by taking them through batteries of tests for the sake of practice and familiarity. Do not try to "teach the test." That is self-defeating, since there are always different questions on every test, and in most cases it is an illegal practice.

You should have your students practice the technique of reading questions from one paper and placing answers in the correct boxes or on the correct lines on another paper, making certain that both the question and the answer have the same number.

You should help them learn how to handle a test-answer sheet, filling in the boxes and providing all the identifying information (name, address, age, etc.) on that sheet and filling in the coded boxes.

You should help students practice on the kinds of content exercises they will find on most tests including:

- Dealing with analogies (simple ones at first and then more complex).
- Finding things that match and things that do not belong together in a group of pictures, words, numbers, etc.
- Answering negative questions.
- Filling in blanks with appropriate words from lists.
- Making "multiple-choice" judgments.
- Reading and following directions.
- Defining words.
- Reading and understanding graphs and maps.
- Finding the next appropriate figures in a sequence.

- Writing a short explanation.
- Writing an informative paragraph.
- Writing a several-paragraph essay on a single topic.

You should provide opportunities for students to practice how to scan a paragraph to find a main idea, skip questions that are too hard and come back to them later. Your students should learn to pause for several deep breaths if they feel panicky. They also ought to be prepared for meeting the time constraints which apply in formal testing situations. Your students ought to learn how to prepare themselves for taking tests, including:

1. Getting a good night's rest the night before.
2. Eating a balanced meal but not overeating.
3. Going to the bathroom before going in to the test site.
4. Bringing necessary things with them, including:
   - An easy-to-eat snack;
   - Several sharpened pencils;
   - Some tissues or a handkerchief;
   - Their eyeglasses, hearing aids, etc.

What is extremely important is that they arrive at the test site on time (early, if possible).

Books full of tests are available in bookstores all across the country. In fact, in most cities you will find that there are coaching courses to help students prepare for taking SAT's as well as legal bar exams, teaching exams, medical exams, and civil service exams. You may wish to become one of these coaches. The Bibliography as well as Appendix E at the back of this book contain lists of manuals and suggestions you may find useful if you plan to offer students help in this test-taking area.

Tutoring For Corporations And Other Businesses

Because our public schools are doing so poor a job these days and because so many of our young people go all through school and are then graduated with very limited basic skills, businesses all across the country are finding that they have to provide basic skills classes for their employees in which they are taught to read, write, spell, compute and communicate correctly. There are fine opportunities for good tutors in these commercial programs. You do not have to wait to see an ad in a newspaper asking for instructors to apply for such positions. It would serve you well to be proactive at this time in selling such services to a company near where you live.

Begin with a letter to the company president describing the service you would like to provide, why you believe such a service would benefit the company as a whole as well as individuals in the company's work force, and the potential cost (per student, per class, or per session) of the instruction you offer.

Ask for some time to discuss additional aspects of the particular program you wish to offer, as well as adding to your program any specifics the corporation feels are lacking in their employees. Indicate that you will call in a few days to set up an appointment.

Carefully prepare for that meeting. Be ready to sell your services in all of the ways we have discussed throughout this manual, especially in the beginning chapters. Review those now.

Working as a tutor in a corporate setting can provide you with a steady income. You can ask to be put on the payroll, or you can decide to come in as a consultant on a free-lance basis. These are options you should discuss with your accountant to determine what would be most profitable for you.

Tutoring Tutors

Offering "How To . . . " classes for potential instructors is another way to earn money as a tutor. There are many out there who may want to become tutors but need some encouragement and self-confidence. You can help them find both of these things. Using a book such as this one as a reference, you can set up sessions to guide those who may wish to tutor.

The first step, as always, would have to be to find clients. As in any other tutoring enterprise, this would mean specialty advertising and word-of-mouth contacting in the community.

Once you have your students, you would lead them through the self-assessment exercises and particular methods for each of the subjects they wish to tutor. Then you could remain a consultant and a mentor to them (on a fee basis) while they are launching their service.

"Speaking" As A Tutoring Possibility

Almost everyone can talk, but there are many people, everywhere, who use the language badly, whose accents or intonations make it diffi-cult for others to understand what they are saying, who do not know or use correct grammar, and who would like to be able to learn to speak standard American English. In addition, there are many people who would like to be able to stand up and speak in public without fear and trembling. These are two different sets of skills, but both offer opportuni-ties to the tutor.

All of the techniques presented in the chapter on teaching English to those speaking foreign languages are applicable when helping our own people to improve the way they speak.

- First the student must be helped to hear the difference between the sounds of the words and sentences he or she produces and the way standard speech sounds. A tape recorder is an invaluable tool in this process.
- The student should use a mirror at every session to watch himself or herself speak.
- Exercises to get the voice out of the nose, to get the tongue placed properly so as to eliminate lisps and dentalizations, and to accent the correct parts of words and the correct words in sentences ought to be included in the training.
- In addition, the student will have to learn the standard pronuncia-tion of words such as ask, oil, mother, car, etc.

Helping people learn how to stand on their feet and make a presenta-tion in public is a different matter. This involves preparation, practice, and opportunity. Unless a person has many opportunities to speak in public, the thought of getting up and addressing an audience will con-tinue to cause anxiety. In this endeavor, opportunity is extremely important. But even more important is having something to say and being clear about what that is. To be sure of that, a student has to learn to prepare. Organizing one's thoughts and jotting notes on what one wishes to say is essential for the novice who wishes to learn to be a public speaker.

Writing an interesting speech, warming up an audience with an appropriate anecdote, establishing eye contact, varying the tone of one's voice, and a host of other techniques can be learned, but students must be helped to realize that public speaking is one of those skills that takes practice and can't be effective without it.

As a tutor, you can bring these messages to students, provide them with opportunities to practice and be there to guide and encourage as they make their presentations.

Chapter 16

EXPANDING YOUR TUTORING BUSINESS

Whether you started your tutoring business with clients you saw and worked with one at a time, or with small groups of clients, you may soon feel the need to expand so that you are offering instruction in more than one area and so that you are not the only tutor working out of your center. In essence, an expanded tutoring business is a school, but a school that offers other than traditional instruction in other than traditional academic areas, along with instruction in the usual academics. Just as the curriculum you would offer in such a center (school) is apt to be unique, so too, the methods you use will probably be non-traditional.

There are many such tutoring services in this country. They can be found in big and small cities and sometimes even in small towns. One company advertises that it has 500 centers nationwide. It is essentially a franchise operation. If you are interested in that kind of affiliation, you can write or call the Sylvan Learning Centers for additional information about their offerings and methods. But a franchise is certainly not your only option should you wish to expand. Neither is an academic tutoring center the only kind that you may want to open. With all we have discussed in this volume, you are surely aware that the field is almost limitless.

There are instrumental music schools, dancing schools, drama schools, crafts schools, art schools, design schools, needlework schools, cooking schools, TV repair schools, auto body schools, schools that offer varieties of subjects in varieties of fields under one roof—all kinds of schools that are operating successfully as learning centers in one part of the country or another. The list could go on and on.

But the crucial decision, no matter what your offerings would be, is whether you wish to run a center. You really must decide whether you are certain that you want to expand from your self-employed status as individual tutor to a new status as an entrepreneur. Do you really want your working days to be devoted to owning and managing a learning center?

If you decide that it is the way you want to move on, there are some practical things for you to begin to do. One of the first is to devise a projected timetable for the expansion. You should determine that by a specific date in the future you would like to be fully operational and then work backwards from that date to the present, inserting into your time-table the steps you know you will have to take along the way. For example, if you wish to be an operational center by the end of January and it is now the beginning of June, you ought to lay out a calendar that looks something like this.

Jan. 31 – Opening Day For Students
Jan 29 – Open House For Community – Catered
Jan 28 –
(Continue listing dates and activities planned for each of the dates.)
June 2 – Make appointment with accountant for review of plan.
June 1 – Construct plan for opening tutoring center.

Working on a sketch like this will help you picture how the conversion from single-person tutor to a learning center manager ought to occur and what big steps must be taken along the way. Planning this way will help you to come to a decision on whether or not you ought to launch such an undertaking. In addition, you ought to develop a checklist for yourself on the advantages and disadvantages of such a conversion. Some of each are presented below for your consideration.

Advantages Of Establishing A Learning Center

There are several very powerful advantages which can serve to influence your thinking concerning the advisability of converting your individual tutoring business into a multi-offering learning center:

- Your income would be steadier since it would no longer depend on whether or not you are in active interaction with clients.
- You can arrange to be paid a steady salary out of the income of the center.
- If you pay yourself a salary you can arrange for the center to provide you with health insurance and other employee benefits.
- You will be able to reach and teach many more clients in many more instructional areas and employ other tutors to work for you.
- Since you will be able to serve many more clients than you could when working alone, you can expect to see much more income

because more students will be able to be taught in small groups as well as individually and this will result in greater earnings per tutoring session.

- As your center becomes known and people begin to develop confidence in your services, less of your effort and time will have to be spent in finding clients. They will begin to find you.
- A permanent address will make your center more easily recognizable.
- Your center will become a familiar place within the community.
- You will have other tutors affiliated with the center who will be available to substitute for you if for some reason you cannot make a session with one of your students.
- You will gain a certain amount of prestige as an owner of a business in the community.
- You will always have a space away from your home in which you can do your own one-to-one and your own small group tutoring.
- You may be able to rent out rooms in your center to other community organizations.

Disadvantages Of Establishing A Learning Center

1. You will be spending much more of your time as a manager and administrator involved with the business aspects of your enterprise than as a tutor directly involved with the teaching-learning situation of your students.
2. You will either have to be responsible for paying salaries or for working out individual consultant contracts with those independent tutors who will be working for you.
3. Your overhead expenses will increase, since you will need larger quarters than those you use as an individual tutor.
   - You will need such additional non-tutoring on site personnel as a secretary and some custodial staff.
   - You will certainly need the services of a lawyer and an accountant.
4. There may be additional county and state small business regulations and even safety regulations besides those you had to meet as a tutor which you will have to conform to in opening a learning center which will be serving the public.
   - Insurances of various kinds
   - Taxes: income, property, social security, other
   - Licenses

These, of course, are only partial lists. They cite only a few examples of the many advantages and disadvantages of establishing a learning center. They are simply illustrative, not by any means all inclusive.

It would be very advantageous if you were to think through your own situation well before you begin to take any further steps and confront those additional pros and cons that you can think of as well as the ones which are listed above. Anticipating difficulties may help keep you from making costly mistakes.

First Steps

Before doing anything as major as opening up a learning center, it would be a smart idea to visit the heads of various private schools and talk to the owner-directors about problems they faced when they were opening their schools. Depending on how you approach them and how close their operations are to the one you are contemplating opening, they may be happy to talk to you or they may suspect that you could well become unwanted competition. Try to select schools to visit which are not in the immediate geographic area in which you plan to open your center. Make appointments, don't just drop in.

You might want to find answers to some of the following questions:

- How much money did they have to invest to get their learning center (school) started?
- Did they have either private or "foundation" financial backing?
- Did they seek a bank loan? Were they successful in obtaining a bank loan? From which bank?
- Did they seek any assistance from the Small Business Administration? Did the SBA help them? How?
- What kinds of obstacles did they have to face that they hadn't anticipated?
- How long has their center been open?
- What would they have done differently if they were starting over?
- What are the major difficulties they still have to deal with today?
- What kind of advice are they willing to give you? What should you be most wary of?
- Are they as successful as they thought they were going to be? What do they consider their greatest success?

Once you have gathered as much practical information as possible from these other entrepreneurs, it is absolutely essential that you sit down and draw up a business plan. It would be a good idea to get help from an accountant in creating such a plan. Refer to your timetable sketch to help you focus on what to plan for. Your business plan will have to include at least the following elements:

1. A decision as to whether to become a corporation, and if so, when.
   - There are costs involved with taking this step.
   - There are forms to be filed on a periodic basis if you are a corporation.
   - There are protections that becoming a corporation offers that you can get no other way. Your accountant should be able to spell these out for you and advise you on what steps to take.
2. A projection of your short-range (six months) and long-range (one year) costs for:
   - Rent (perhaps mortgage payments and property taxes) and utilities
   - Building services (cleaning and physical maintenance)
   - Purchase or rental of furniture and business machines including duplicators, computers, typewriters
   - Software and other supplies
   - Staff salaries (based on staff-student ratios)
   - Other personnel expenses
     a. Personnel benefits
     b. Insurance and fees
   - Unanticipated expenses.
3. A projection of your short-range and long-range income goals which includes consideration of the number of students your center will have to serve at specific per-session rates if you are going to be able to meet those goals.
4. A projection of short- and long-range realistic profit objectives.
5. Potential plans for expansion into other income-producing activities as well as tutoring such as:
   - Selling books and supplies
   - Selling software (computer and other)
   - Selling logoed shirts, caps, socks and other goods
   - Renting out rooms for other purposes when they are not being used by learning center personnel.

6. A projection of startup costs and a determination of whether you will need outside capital to get your center started. If so:
   - How much?
   - For how long?
   - Who might be likely creditors?

Next Steps

If after learning all you can about how others have fared in the business and, after creating a potential timetable and a business projection (do this with the help of your accountant), you still feel that you want to expand your tutoring service and turn it into a learning center, there are a number of next steps to take:

1. You will want to be in touch with the Small Business Administration to get their assistance if you need startup money or planning assistance.
2. You will want to do some investigating to discover whether there might be some "grant" money available to you (private or government).
3. You will want to locate a building with adequate parking, good sanitary facilities and a rent or purchase price that you can manage; and you will want to begin to make plans for outfitting it as a learning center. (This should be on your timetable.)
   - It should have adaptable small rooms which can serve as tutorial rooms.
   - It should have several larger rooms which can serve as group meeting rooms for teaching games, crafts, dance, studio arts, workshops, etc.
   - It should have rooms that can serve as offices.
   - It should have bathrooms.
   - It should have adequate parking facilities.
4. You will need to plan your advertising campaigns:
   - For attracting tutors;
   - For attracting clients;
   - For attracting other personnel.

Your Learning Center And The Community

A good way to start, once you have things in place and are ready to accept clients, is to hold an open house for the community. Invite people to come see your facility and meet some of your tutors. You can host such gatherings several times during your early years of operation. Letting people know what your learning center looks like and how it functions will serve to alert them to your service and will, at the same time, advertise the fact that the rooms in the center are available to be rented for other groups' functions if and when you have space available.

Once you are in the learning center business you will want to keep your rooms in use as much of the time as possible so it will be in your best interest to find ways to stay in touch with the needs of the community.

You will want, periodically, to review all of the subjects you are offering. When you do this it will be in your interest to take account of what you learn about the needs of the community for assistance in all learning areas, as well as how the community is growing or otherwise changing, and what emerging needs may be. Your reviews should always include examination of the following areas:

- The academics including: reading, writing, enrichment, arithmetic, algebra, geometry, chemistry, biology, physics, the social studies, foreign languages, English as a foreign language, study skills, test-taking skills and coaching courses for such tests as the graduate equivalency degree examination and the national teacher examination.
- The homemaking crafts including: needlework, knitting, crocheting, flower arranging, ceramics, woodworking, pottery, sculpture, leatherwork, jewelry making.
- Other homemaking pursuits including: cooking, baking, decorating, sewing.
- Shopwork including: automobile mechanics, carpentry, plumbing, metalwork, electricity and electronics, TV repair, radio repair, VCR repair, household repairs, woodworking.
- Computer workshops including: the computer and computer languages, using many varieties of computer software, enhancing the PC you own (hardware), enhancing the PC you own (software), computer languages.
- The arts including: sculpture (clay, metal, wood and stone), painting (watercolor and oil), music (vocal and instrumental), dance

(modern, ballet, tap, clogging, ballroom), drama, creative writing (fiction, drama, poetry).
- Other skills including: speech and speech making, the signing language of the deaf.
- Games including: bridge, mah-jong, chess, backgammon, go, scrabble, pinochle, etc.
- Body-building pursuits including: aerobics, gymnastics, yoga, diet and nutrition classes.
- Pre-school instruction for toddlers including: story telling, finger painting, block building, singing, dancing, rhythm instruments, etc.
- Business subjects including: word processing, shorthand, business machines, bookkeeping, etc.
- Other instruction.

Of course, you may not wish to use your center for all these activities. And even if you begin by offering some things, along the way you may wish to change what you are offering. The choice of specialties will be yours. But as you can see from the quick list above, which is extensive but by no means all inclusive, there are a great many choices of activities on which you can build a learning center.

Chapter 17

HUMOR AND WISDOM

There are many humorous anecdotes told about teaching, tutoring, the relationship between the instructor and the learner, and the whole process of education. In a book devoted to tutoring, it seems like a good idea to offer a few of these wise words and stories so you may have them at your command if and when you need to lighten a moment.

- Almost all parents would like their children to be in the top 10% of their class, but 90% cannot make it.
- Maybe we cannot do everything at once, but we surely can do one thing at once.
- A wise college dean once said that his school was a storehouse of knowledge because the freshmen brought in so much and the seniors took out so little.
- One of the difficulties with education today is that it so often covers ground without cultivating anything in it.
- A father was scolding his son for bringing home a report card full of "C's" and "D's." He asked his son why it was that Johnny (his best friend) managed to get mostly "A's." "Oh," the youngster answered. "Johnny's different. He has very bright parents."
- "Do you like going to school?" the grandmother asked her granddaughter.

  "I do," the young girl answered. "And I like coming home, too. I just don't like to have to stay there all day."
- It's hard for a child to keep a chip on his shoulder if you encourage him to take a bow.
- There really is something which costs more than education today—the lack of it.
- "I don't care what your father told you," the teacher insisted, "money is not considered this country's biggest export."
- Remember the lesson Confucius taught—a journey of a thousand miles begins with a single step.

147

- The tutor asked her student to write a sentence using both the words first and last. The student, after pondering for a few moments wrote, "This is the first time I have done something like this and I hope it will be the last."
- Trying to get across the idea of addition, the tutor asked the student what he would have if he had five pennies in one pocket and six in the other.
  "Someone else's pants on," the boy replied.
- One tutor said to another, "If I were Rockefeller, I'd be richer than Rockefeller."
  The other tutor asked, "How could that be?"
  The first tutor answered, "I'd do a little tutoring on the side."
- Genius, that quality that dazzles human eyes, Is oft but perspiration in disguise.
- "How can I show my appreciation for all you've done for my son?" the parent asked the tutor.
  In scholarly fashion the tutor replied, "Sir, ever since the Phoenicians invented money there has been only one answer to that question."
- "Tell me," the young tutor asked the tutor who'd been at it for a long time, "how do you teach participles?" The response was immediate, and a single word at that. "Beautifully."
- It is very difficult to raise a student up by calling him down.
- The people joked about the foolish boy who always took the nickel when people offered him a nickel or a dime. One day someone told him the dime was worth twice as much as the nickel.
  "I know," said the boy. "But if I took the dime people would stop offering me money."
- Because we are so anxious to give everyone a college degree, we often fail to give too many an education.
- In an initial interview about her ten-year-old son, a mother was telling the tutor about her family. She said her thirteen-year-old son was in the county reform school, her fifteen-year-old daughter was in a program for the retarded, and her eighteen-year-old son was in Harvard.
  "Really?" the tutor said. "What is he studying?"
  "Nothing," the mother replied. "They're studying him."
- Your student will remember your compliment a lot longer than any scolding you may give him.

- Democracy is based upon the absolute conviction that there are extraordinary possibilities in the most ordinary people.

Some Closing Words

It is easy to see that there is a wealth of opportunity in the community for anyone who wishes to earn money by tutoring. The work is there to be had.

POTENTIAL FOR EARNING (In Dollars)
FOR ONE-ON-ONE TUTORING

Per Session Fee @	Sessions Per Day	Daily Income	Days Per Week	Weekly Income	Weeks Per Year	Yearly Income
15	4	60	5	300	50	$15,000
20	4	80	5	400	50	20,000
25	4	100	5	500	50	25,000
30	4	120	5	600	50	30,000
35	4	140	5	700	50	35,000
40	4	160	5	800	50	40,000

NOTE: $35.00 per session is the average rate in many towns.

FOR GROUP INSTRUCTION
(Potential)

Per Student Per Session	Minimum # Of Students	Sessions Per Week	Weekly Income	Weeks Per Year	Yearly Income
$5	5	1	25	50	1,250
5	10	1	50	50	2,500
5	10	2	100	50	5,000
5	10	5	250	50	12,500
10	5	1	50	50	2,500
10	10	1	100	50	5,000
10	10	2	200	50	10,000
10	10	5	500	50	25,000
12	10	5	600	50	30,000

NOTE: The figures presented above are for illustrative purposes to demonstrate potential earnings in tutoring. Length of sessions may vary from 45 minutes when working with an individual student on remediation, to as long as two hours when working with a group on something like bridge or square dancing.

People are waiting to be informed of the availability of services. The way you advertise and the frequency with which you advertise are the keys for bringing them to you. Your individual success in helping them to learn will be the single most important factor in keeping clients coming.

Good luck!

APPENDICES

This section contains examples and practical advice. References to these pages can be found in the body of the text.

SAMPLE RESUME FOR APPLYING FOR A JOB
(NOT FOR TUTORING)

JOSEPH P. HOWARD
134 WEST 85 STREET
MIDLAND, NEW JERSEY, 07900
(201) 464-3456

EMPLOYMENT GOAL	Teaching auto mechanics and the essentials of small-engine repair as a per-session or part-time employee in a in a high school or a community college.
EMPLOYMENT HISTORY	Owned and operated JPH AUTO REPAIR SHOP from 1965 to 1988—Plainfield, N.J.—Retired
	Line Supervisor—MACK TRUCK, INC. 1955–1965—Plainfield, New Jersey
EDUCATION	Midland Park High School—1952
	Union County College, New Jersey 1952–1955 Associate Degree in Auto Mechanics
SKILLS	Experienced in all aspects of automobile engine repair and all aspects of running an auto repair shop.
EXPERIENCE	Served as a substitute shop teacher in six New Jersey High schools during 1988–89.
	Instructor in Central Community School's Auto Mechanics course during summer of 1989.
QUALIFICATIONS	Hold a substitute teacher's certificate and have applied for full teaching certificate with "life experience" credit and three-year degree.
REFERENCES	MR. HARRY HARROW—PRINCIPAL Central Community School 921 Main Street North Unionville, N.J. 07900
AVAILABILITY	Immediate.

A Few Helpful Comments Concerning Design Of A Resume

The person who will see your resume is a potential employer. What he or she will be looking for is the ESSENTIAL information about you in reference to the position you would like to hold. Because of this, you should be careful to include everything about you that could make you more attractive in an employer's eyes for the particular position you want, and include nothing that doesn't apply.

For instance, JOSEPH P. HOWARD might be a par golfer, an outstanding father, and a whiz at mathematics, but he wants to teach auto mechanics. That is why his resume sticks to what might sell him as an auto-mechanics teacher. Other things about him might come up in his employment interview if he is called for one, but it is the resume that determines whether or not he will be called.

The resume, whenever possible, should be on one page. If you have more to say, have it typeset so that it will still fit on one page. It should be organized so that the eye can move quickly from point to point and find needed information without a struggle.

Headings should be relevant and should stand out. Spelling should be perfect. Typos should be eliminated. The paper should be substantial stock. The printing should be easy to read. Your resume is your introduction. Make it a good one.

Appendix B

SPREAD SHEET

(DATE)

	JAN	FEB	MAR	APR	MAY	JUN	JUL	AUG	SEPT	OCT	NOV	DEC	TOT.
101													
102													
103													
104													
105													
TOT													
201													
202													
203													
204													
301													
302													
303													
304													
305													
306													
401													
402													
403													
404													

SPREAD SHEET (*Continued*)

(DATE)

	JAN	FEB	MAR	APR	MAY	JUN	JUL	AUG	SEPT	OCT	NOV	DEC	TOT.
501													
502													
503													
504													
505													
506													
507													
601													
602													
603													
604													
701													
702													
703													
704													
TOT.													
NET													

NOTE: See Chart of Accounts, pages 46 and 47 for the meaning of each of these
numbers.

Appendix C

THANK YOU LETTER

NOTE: Use your stationery with your own letterhead if you have it. If not, use plain white paper and type in your return address as below. This sample letter may be modified as needed to send to clergy and others you have visited.

2213 East 22 Street
Plainfield, N.J. 07060
April 23, 199

Dr. K.R. Fellows—Principal
Central Community School
3434 Washington Street
Union, N.J. 07077

Dear Dr. Fellows:

I very much appreciate the time you spent with me on Tuesday afternoon. Walking through your school with you and listening to your explanations concerning what is unique to Central Community School, what it offers and which community needs it fills, was both interesting and instructive for me.

Although I am not seeking employment other than as a private tutor right now, I would be grateful if you would keep the enclosed resume in your personnel files. Should you seek an instructor with my qualifications in the future, please call me.

Once again, thank you for your time.

Sincerely,

Enc: Resume
      Business Card

NOTE: Rather than the second paragraph above, or prior to it, you may wish to use the following:

I was especially impressed with [cite one or more of the particular things you saw]. You indeed have reason to be proud of such a program.

WORDING OF SAMPLE ADS
FOR GETTING CLIENTS

General

Have you always wanted to . . . ?

What is holding you back?

We can help you. FREE CONSULTATION.

Call (222) 222-2222

Monday through Saturday — 8:30 A.M. to 8:30 P.M.

NOTE: In the space next to "Have you always wanted to . . ." use phrases like " . . . read silently and aloud without difficulty?" " . . . be the best cook in your family?" " . . . understand how your car engine works?" " . . . speak and understand English?" " . . . do Math without fear of making mistakes?"

For School Age Students

STUDENTS — PARENTS

Would you like to make this the most successful school year you have ever had?

We can help you to make it that way. We can help you learn:

- How to make the most of your study time
- How to take tests without fear
- How to get the most from your classes.

We provide specific instruction in ....

Come see us for a FREE CONSULTATION. Call (222) 222-2222

Monday through Saturday — 8:30 A.M. to 8:30 P.M.

NOTE: What is important in an ad is that it be eye-catching, provide essential information, and stimulate enough interest to make a potential client want to call.

158

Appendix E

SUGGESTIONS FOR HELPING STUDENTS DEVELOP TEST TAKING SKILLS

None of these suggestions include "teaching the test." That is self-defeating and, in most cases, illegal.

1. Have students practice the following techniques:
   a. Reading questions from one paper and placing answers in the correct boxes or on the correct line on another paper making certain that both the question and the answer have the same number.
   b. Filling in boxes or parallel lines on a prepared answer sheet corresponding to numbered questions on a test sheet.
   c. Providing all identifying information (name, address, age, etc.) on an answer sheet and filling in coded boxes.
2. Provide practice for students in:
   a. Dealing with analogies (simple at first and then more complex).
   b. Finding things that match and things that do not belong in a group of pictures, words, numbers, etc.
   c. Answering negative questions.
   d. Filling in blanks with appropriate words from lists.
   e. Making "multiple-choice" judgments.
   f. Reading and following directions.
   g. Defining words.
   h. Finding the next appropriate figures in a sequence.
3. Provide opportunities for students to learn:
   a. To scan a paragraph to find a main idea.
   b. To skip questions that are too hard and come back to them later.
   c. To read and understand graphs and maps.
   d. To pause for several deep breaths if they feel panicky.
   e. To understand the time constraints for formal tests.
4. Help students learn how to prepare themselves for tests:
   a. Get a good night's rest the night before a test.
   b. Eat a balanced meal, but don't overeat.
   c. Bring along an easy-to-eat snack.
   d. Go to the bathroom before going in to the test site.
   e. Bring several sharpened pencils.
   f. Bring a handkerchief.
   g. Bring eyeglasses, hearing aids, etc.

    h. Be on time.
5. Give students practice in:
    a. Writing a short explanation.
    b. Writing an informative paragraph.
    c. Writing a several-paragraph essay on a single topic.

SUGGESTED LESSON PLAN FORM

LESSON PLAN FORM

LESSON WITH
STUDENT: _____ DATE: _____

INTERACTIVE REVIEW FROM PREVIOUS LESSON (10 MINUTES): _____

_____

_____

NEW MATERIAL FOR THIS SESSION—LIST:_____

_____

_____

_____

ACTIVITIES AND CHALLENGES FOR THIS SESSION: _____

_____

_____

_____

_____

PERFORMANCE EVALUATION AND REVIEW OF THIS SESSION: _____

_____

_____

NOTES FOR NEXT SESSION: _____

_____

_____

Appendix G

SOME ALPHABET GAMES

1. "A" my name is "Alma" (Andy) and my husband's (wife's) name is "Alan"; we come from "America" and we sell "apples." (The student can take this all through the alphabet—"B" my name is . . . ; and my husband's name is . . . ; we come from . . . ; and we sell . . . etc.)

2. I'm going to Jerusalem and in my bag I'm taking "apples."
   I'm going to Jerusalem and in my bag I'm taking "apples and bananas."
   I'm going to Jerusalem and in my bag I'm taking "apples, bananas and coffee."
   I'm going to Jerusalem and in my bag I'm taking "apples, bananas, coffee and dates."
   (Continue down through the alphabet taking turns with the student and repeating the full contents of the bag with every turn. You might want to help the student "write" and then "read" what is in the bag as it becomes fuller.

3. How long a list can you make of words that describe?
   Put each list in alphabetical order.
   Mary is . . . (tall, pretty, young, silly, etc.)
   John is . . .
   The dog is . . .
   The teacher is . . .
   The TV program is . . .
   The car is . . .
   My house is . . .
   Today is . . .
   This game is . . .

4. Rhyming words: Take turns with your student naming and writing all the "and," "end," "ink," "it," "ack," etc., words you can think of. Write them down. Your student gets a point for each word (no nonsense words) and you get half a point for each word.

5. Cut a full-page picture from a magazine. Have your student label each object in the picture with the first letter of its name. Then try the same thing with the last sounded letter of its name.

6. As quickly as you can fill in what is missing:

   - a＿＿d
   - k＿＿＿o   (Real beginnings of words only)
   - v＿＿＿z   • ca＿＿ci
   - y＿＿＿＿t   • fl＿＿fu

162

- p_____l   • sp__sw
- e_____a

7. Write the following:

- All letters with tails (j, y, g, p, q)
- All letters with high tops (b, d, f, h, k, l, t)
- All short rounded letters (a, c, e, o, s, u)
- All pointed letters (k, v, w, x, z)
- All short hilly letters (m, n, r)
- All dotted letters (i, j)
- All crossed letters (f, t, x)

8. Sounds of the vowels: Under each word, make a list of all the words you can think of (in one minute) in which the same vowel sounds the same way:

- A: cat; cape; cart; saw; alone; . . .
- E: see; her; beg; . . .
- I: big; bite; . . .
- O: bog; cow; boy; bone; boot; . . .
- U: cut; cure; put; . . .

9. List the consonants that change their sounds when followed by different vowels (c, g, . . .). List the consonant combinations often found in English (th, ch, sh, ck, lk, st, sch, ph, gh, ght, cr, pr, psych, wh, ly, fl, fr, etc.) Put these into alphabetical order.

Appendix H

SUGGESTED WRITING ASSIGNMENTS

For Children

1. If I had a hundred dollars right now I would . . .
2. If I could take a trip . . . (Note: There are endless numbers of additional "If I . . ." assignments leading to one or two additional sentences for completion.)
3. I woke up one day to find that I had changed into a . . . (Go on to tell what happened next.)
4. I never want to have to . . . because.
5. I know a (man, woman, boy, girl, dog, cat) who . . .
6. Write me a note telling me why you . . .
7. Describe your favorite game or toy.
8. Paint a word-picture of your (friend, mother, father, etc.).

For Adults

1. If I could change the world the first thing I would do would be . . .
2. If I were truly rich I would . . . (See No. 2 note, above).
3. When I am (angry, happy, discouraged, hopeful) I show it by . . .
4. The kind of (music, stories, entertainment, work, etc.) I like best is . . . because . . .
5. Write me a note telling me why you won't be able to . . .
6. I heard them knocking on the door and I . . . (Write at least 100 words.)
7. It was true. I didn't know (where I was; who I was; who he was; where we were; etc.), but the sun was going down. (Write 200 words.)

For Either Children Or Adults

1. Make a list of your favorite ten TV programs. Copy them from the newspaper or a TV guide.
2. The five foods I like best for (dinner, snacks, breakfast, lunch) are:
3. I love TV programs that . . .
4. I despise TV programs that . . .
5. I never saw a tree that had so many colors. The trunk was . . . . The branches were . . . . The leaves were . . .
6. The kinds of stories I like best are . . . because . . .
7. Describe one room in your house so that I would recognize it if I came to visit.
8. You are going shopping in three different kinds of stores. Write down the kinds of stores you are going to shop in. Make a list of at least seven items you are going

to buy in each of the stores. (Students can check spelling in the dictionary if you believe them capable. They can also alphabetize their lists.)

9. Write a letter to . . . telling them about . . .

Appendix I

A FUNCTIONAL READING WORD LIST
FOR ADULTS*

a	beauty	children	dollar	female
able	beautiful	church	done	finance
about	because	cigarette	don't	fine
accept	been	city	door	finish
account	beer	class	down	fire
add	before	clean	dress	first
address	begin	cleaner	drive	fish
admit	began	clothes	driver	floor
after	belong	coat	dry	following
age	benefit	coffee	during	food
ahead	beside	cold	duty	foot
age	besides	color		for
air	best	come	earn	former
all	better	company	east	forward
allow	between	Co.	easy	found
also	big	complete	edge	free
altogether	bill	condition	egg	freedom
A.M. a.m.	birth	continue	electric	Friday
American	black	corner	electricity	Fri.
amount	block	cost	emergency	from
amt.	board	could	employ	front
an	boat	cream	employment	full
and	body	credit	enter	furnish
any	box	cross	equipment	furniture
apartment	bread	crossing	equip.	
apt.	break		escape	game
application	breakfast	daily	establish	gas
are	building	danger	est.	gasoline
area	bldg.	date	estate	get
arm	bus	day	estimate	give

*From Hanson, Marie, and Bessey, Barbra: *Tutor Training Guide—English As A Second Language.* A Set of Five Modules for Use in Training Volunteer ESL Tutors. Portland, Oregon: Chemeketa Community College Press, 1988, Reproduced by permission.

army	business	dealer	etc.	glass
as	but	delivery	evening	go
ask	butter	department	eve.	goes
at	buy	dept.	ever	good
automobile	by	dependent	every	group
auto		did	exceed	guard
automatic	call	dime	exit	
available	can	dinner	experience	had
avenue	car	disability	express	hair
ave.	care	distance	eye	half
away	case	district		hand
	cause	do	fat	hardware
back	charge	doctor	feet	has
bar	check	Dr.	ft.	have
he	large	minute	only	radio
head	last	min.	open	rate
hear	law	Miss	opposite	real
heart	lease	modern	or	reason
heat	leave	Monday	order	record
height	left	Mon.	other	red
ht.	license	money	our	register
help	life	month	out	rent
her	like	mo.	over	repair
here	limit	monthly	own	residential
high	line	more	owner	rest
him	liquor	mortgage		restaurant
his	live	most	page	return
home	loan	motor	paid	right
hospital	local	move	pd.	road
hosp.	long	Mr.	paint	roof
hot	loss	Mrs.	paper	room
hour	low	much	park	
hour	low	much	park	
hr.		must	part	safe
house	machine	my	pass	safety
how	made		pay	said
husband	mail	name	payment	sale
	make	narrow	pmt.	sandwiches
I	male	national	period	satisfaction
ice	man	nationality	person	satisfactory
if	manager	near	pick	Saturday
in	mgr.	need	picture	Sat.
include	many	new	place	save
income	mark	next	plain	saw
individual	married	nickel	plan	say

information	material	night	please	school
info.	maximum	nite	P.M. p.m.	security
installment	may	no	point	see
insurance	me	north	police	self
into	mean	not	present	service
is	means	now	price	sex
it	meat	number	private	shall
	mechanical	no.	prohibit	she
jeans	medical	nurse	prompt	shoe
join	meeting		promptly	shop
joint	member	occupation	property	should
just	men	of	provide	show
	mental	off	public	shut
keep	metal	office		side
kind	mile	oil	quality	sign
kitchen	military	old	quart	signal
know	milk	on	quarter	signature
known	mind	one	quiet	since
single	their	Wednesday		
size	them	Wed.		
slow	there	week	A FEW ADDITIONAL WORDS	
small	these	wk.		
smoke	they	weight	accountant	
snow	this	wgt.	baseball	
so	those	welfare	boy	
social	through	were	cent	
society	thru	west	circle	
sold	Thursday	what	computer	
some	Thurs.	when	cup	
son	ticket	where	daughter	
south	time	which	dentist	
so.	tire	who	father	
special	to	wife	football	
speed	too	will	freezer	
stamp	tool	window	girl	
stand	trade	with	golf	
start	traffic	woman	highway	
state	truck	women	key	
station	Tuesday	word	menu	
stay	Tues.	work	moon	
steel	turn	write	mother	
stock	two		parent	
stone	type	year	penny	
stop		yr.	pint	
store	under	yellow	read	

street	union	yes	refrigerator
st.	unite	yet	saucer
strike	up	you	sky
suit	United	your	stars
such	States	yours	stove
Sunday	upon		sun
Sun.	use	zero	tablespoon
supply			tbs.
system	vegetable		teaspoon
	vehicle		tsp.
take			
tavern	wait		all the colors
tax	walk		all the months
telephone	want		all the numbers
tel.	war		
television	was		
TV	wash		
term	watch		
than	water		
that	way		
the	we		

Appendix J

ADDITION-SUBTRACTION TABLE

0	1	2	3	4	5	6	7	8	9	10	11	12
1	2	3	4	5	6	7	8	9	10	11	12	13
2	3	4	5	6	7	8	9	10	11	12	13	14
3	4	5	6	7	8	9	10	11	12	13	14	15
4	5	6	7	8	9	10	11	12	13	14	15	16
5	6	7	8	9	10	11	12	13	14	15	16	17
6	7	8	9	10	11	12	13	14	15	16	17	18
7	8	9	10	11	12	13	14	15	16	17	18	19
8	9	10	11	12	13	14	15	16	17	18	19	20
9	10	11	12	13	14	15	16	17	18	19	20	21
10	11	12	13	14	15	16	17	18	19	20	21	22
11	12	13	14	15	16	17	18	19	20	21	22	23
12	13	14	15	16	17	18	19	20	21	22	23	24

Try several examples: 12 − 5; 7 + 8; 18 − 4; 24 − 9.

Review instructions in the text for how these algorithms can be solved on the table.

NUMBER LINE

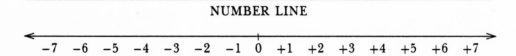

−7 −6 −5 −4 −3 −2 −1 0 +1 +2 +3 +4 +5 +6 +7

Appendix K

MULTIPLICATION-DIVISION TABLE

1	2	3	4	5	6	7	8	9	10	11	12
2	4	6	8	10	12	14	16	18	20	22	24
3	6	9	12	15	18	21	24	27	30	33	36
4	8	12	16	20	24	28	32	36	40	44	48
5	10	15	20	25	30	35	40	45	50	55	60
6	12	18	24	30	36	42	48	54	60	66	72
7	14	21	28	35	42	49	56	63	70	77	84
8	16	24	32	40	48	56	64	72	80	88	96
9	18	27	36	45	54	63	72	81	90	99	108
10	20	30	40	50	60	70	80	90	100	110	120
11	22	33	44	55	66	77	88	99	110	121	132
12	24	36	48	60	72	84	96	108	120	132	144

Review the instructions in the chapter on how to use this table in multiplying, dividing and counting.

THE DECIMAL SYSTEM
AND OTHER BASE SYSTEMS

1. Decimal system—Base ten:

thous-ands	hund-reds	tens	units	.	tenths	hund-reths	thous-enths	ten thous.
9	9	9	9	.	9	9	9	9

9,999.9999

This number would be read as nine thousand nine hundred ninety nine and nine thousand nine hundred ninety nine ten thousandths.

7,654,876,521.09

This number would be read seven billion, six hundred fifty four million, eight hundred seventy six thousand, five hundred twenty one and nine hundreths. In these times of huge budget deficits, it might be well to help your students learn how to read and understand numbers as large as these.

2. Base two: (This is the system used by computers.)
   - Only two digits may be used, a zero and a one. (In base ten we use ten digits, a zero and one through nine.)
   - Anything larger than one (1), like a two (2), would have to be exchanged and put into the next place, just as in base ten we exchange anything larger than a nine and put it into the next place.
   - The place values for base two are as follows:

sixty fours	thirty-twos	six-teens	eights	fours	twos	ones
1	1	1	1	1	1	1
1	0	1	0	1	0	1

   - The top number, 1111111, is the same as the quantity

     $64 + 32 + 16 + 8 + 4 + 2 + 1$ or 127 in base ten.

   - The second number, 1010101, is the same as the quantity

     $64 + 16 + 4 + 1$ or 85 in base ten.

   - The next five columns to the left after "64's" are "128's," "256's," "512's," "1024," "2048." (To establish the value of the remaining columns, continue multiplying the last number by two.)

- Thus, our base ten 2,501, would be $(1 \times 2048) + (0 \times 1024) + (0 \times 512) + (1 \times 256) + (1 \times 128) + (1 \times 64) + (0 \times 32) + (0 \times 16) + (0 \times 8) + (0 \times \frac{1}{8} 4) + (0 \times 2) + (1 \times 1)$ or as written in base two, 100111000101. These numbers look familiar to us these days because computers print them on many things.

Helping your students to translate numbers from one base system to another provides them with practice in multiplication, subtraction and addition in a way that is more fun than chore.

Appendix M

NUMERALS

Cardinal	Arabic	Ordinal	Roman
one	1	first	I
two	2	second	II
three	3	third	III
four	4	fourth	IV
five	5	fifth	V
six	6	sixth	VI
seven	7	seventh	VII
eight	8	eighth	VIII
nine	9	ninth	IX
ten	10	tenth	X
eleven	11	eleventh	XI
twelve	12	twelfth	XII
thirteen	13	thirteenth	XIII
fourteen	14	fourteenth	XIV
fifteen	15	fifteenth	XV
sixteen	16	sixteenth	XVI
seventeen	17	seventeenth	XVII
eighteen	18	eighteenth	XVIII
nineteen	19	nineteenth	XIX
twenty	20	twentieth	XX
twenty-one	21	twenty-first	XXI
twenty-five	25	twenty-fifth	XXV
twenty-nine	29	twenty-ninth	XXIX
thirty	30	thirtieth	XXX
forty	40	fortieth	XL
fifty	50	fifieth	L
sixty	60	sixtieth	LX
seventy	70	seventieth	LXX
eighty	80	eightieth	LXXX
ninety	90	ninetieth	XC
one hundred	100	one hundreth	C
four hundred	400	four hundreth	CD
five hundred	500	five hundreth	D
eight hundred	800	eight hundreth	DCCC
nine hundred	900	nine hundreth	CM

one thousand	1000	one thousandth	M
two thousand	2000	two thousandth	MM
ten thousand	10000	ten thousandth	$\overline{\text{X}}$
one hundred thousand			$\overline{\text{C}}$
one million			$\overline{\text{M}}$

Appendix N

SUGGESTED WORDINGS FOR ADVERTISEMENTS AS A TUTOR

NOTE: These are written for an ESL tutor but can be adapted easily to advertise any other kind of tutoring as well.

1. I am teaching English to those whose native language is not English. Call 222-2222.
2. Whether or not you can read and write in another language — if you want to learn English, I can help you. Call 222-2222.
3. Learn to speak, read and write English. Private lessons. Call 222-2222.
4. Experienced instructor is offering private or group lessons in English for non-native speakers. Learn to speak, read and write. Learn American customs. Call 222-2222.
5.

LEARN ENGLISH QUICKLY

Lessons in: Speaking
Reading
Writing
Shopping
Conversing
Traveling

Learn American customs.
Learn to understand what you are hearing.
Get help in dealing with the practical problems that you face.

Call 222-2222

6. Have you always wanted to . . . ? Now is the time to learn how. Private lessons or group instruction. Call 222-2222.

Appendix O

SUGGESTED ADVERTISING COPY
FOR TUTORING COMPUTERS AND
OTHER PRACTICAL SKILLS

1. Are you willing to spend the rest of your life in fear? Are you afraid of a little box with the small screen? Are you in awe of all the people who can use computers?

    Isn't this the time to take a risk?

    Take a risk!

    Come learn how to use a computer and stop being afraid.
    Call 222-2222 for a free, introductory session.

2.
    The twenty-first century is almost here.
    It will be the age of the computer.
    Don't be caught unprepared.

    LEARN HOW TO USE A COMPUTER

    Private instruction.
    Call 222-2222 for a free demonstration.

3. **COME WORK IN CARRIE'S KITCHEN**

    Learn how to prepare gourmet meals with everyday produce.
    Wonderful recipes—New ways to use kitchen tools.
    Menus for special diets.

    Small classes with a great deal of individual attention.
    Call today for a free demonstration lesson. 222-2222.

4. **FLOWER ARRANGING IS AN ART**

    Come learn to be an artist.

    Call 222-2222

PLACES WHERE INFORMATION CONCERNING CULTURAL DIFFERENCES MAY BE OBTAINED

- The Center For Applied Linguistics, P.O. Box 37422, Washington, D.C. 20013
- United States Department of Education Refugee Materials Center, 324 East 11 Street, 9th Floor, Kansas City, Missouri, 64106

GLOSSARY

The words listed below appear in the text or in the Appendices and are defined here in a manner which comes as close as possible to the way they have been used in the text. These are sometimes only partial dictionary definitions. Sentences are added to illustrate how the words are used.

A

ABBREVIATED — Cut short. Curtailed. Used in reference to decreasing time devoted to a task, shortening a word or replacing dropped letters with an apostrophe. "She *abbreviated* the words do not to make the word don't."

ABUNDANT — Plentiful. A lot more than just enough. "Students were out there in *plentiful* numbers."

ACADEMIC — Referring to or related to schools and colleges and the subject matter (curriculum) they offer the student. Sometimes used to mean scholarly. "The *academic* subjects were the ones on which she chose to concentrate."

ACCORDION FILE — A sturdy folder or an envelope with many pleated folds that permit it to expand to several times its original size and accommodate a great many papers. "The records of the company were temporarily kept in an *accordion file.*"

ADHERE — Stick to something like an idea or an ideal. Obey a rule or regulation. "They try to *adhere* to the spirit as well as to the letter of the law."

ADMINISTER — To manage. To oversee and take charge of the conduct of something. "He took great pains to be sure to *administer* the test fairly."

ADMONITION — A warning, generally about something that ought not to be done. "Responding to the *admonition* of the principal, no one cut classes that day.

ADVERTISING — Letting something be known. A process by which a message is brought to the attention of others. "The way tutors attract their clients is through well-designed *advertising* campaigns."

ADVOCATES — Takes a stand in favor of a way of thinking or a particular point of view. "He *advocates* an eclectic approach to the teaching of reading."

AESTHETIC — Artisticly pleasing primarily because of its beauty or appeal to the senses. "The school halls were decorated with student paintings which created an *aesthetic* atmosphere."

AFFILIATED — Associated with or joined with, generally with reference to business.

"If you become *affiliated* with a corporation, you may earn more money for tutoring."

ALGORISM — A format used for working on an arithmetic, an algebraic, or other mathematical problem. "The *algorism* used for the addition and subtraction of fractions is not generally used for other processes."

ALMANAC — A publication (usually annual) containing various data, particularly that having to do with dates and times — especially timely information pertinent to the year of publication. "The farmer's *almanac* predicts the weather for a year or more at a time."

AMBIDEXTERITY — The ability to use both hands to perform tasks with equal ease and equal competence. "*Ambidexterity* was the gift the switch-hitter brought to the home town baseball team."

ANALOGIES — A particular likeness among things which in other ways may be quite unalike. "Test takers are often faced with finding *analogies* in such questions as: a pear is to a tree as a blueberry is to a ——."

ANTECEDENT — An event, word, or cause that came before the occurrence at hand. "We generally use a pronoun as an *antecedent* to a verb when we are conjugating the verb."

APPLICABLE — Something that applies or can be used in a given situation. "Find a synonym that would be *applicable* in that sentence."

ARRAY — A regular arrangement of numbers or objects. "That grid presented us with an *array* of even numbers."

ASCENDING — Going upward. Mounting. Increasing in a particular order in the way numbers do, with regular intervals between them. "She listed the Roman numerals on the board in *ascending* order."

ASCI — A universal computer language, formulated on a base two system, permitting computers to interact with one another. "My computer sent the message to the data bank in *ASCI* though I had entered it in English."

ASPECT — An appearance or a look or a facet of an object or of a situation. "Be sure you have examined every *aspect* of the problem before you take the big step."

ASSESSMENT — A weighing or an evaluation of a performance or a person. Sometimes a kind of tax. "Once you have made an *assessment* of the situation, you will know what to do."

ASSET — An advantage or a resource or a natural talent. Something that is in one's favor. "A good education is an *asset* to someone who wants to tutor math."

ASTRONOMY — The scientific study of the stars and outer space. "The speaker who lectured at the museum made the science of *astronomy* sound exciting as a field of study."

ASYMMETRICAL — Uneven. Not the same on both sides. Used in mathematics as the opposite of symmetry. "The multi-sided building was obviously *asymmetrical.*"

ATLAS — A book of maps and geographical explanations including figures on population, sizes of towns, cities, states, countries; topography and other physical characteristics are generally included. "The *atlas* contained three maps showing elevations of land beneath the seas."

ATTRIBUTED — To regard something as characteristic of someone or something;

to consider to have been the cause. "They *attributed* the success of the student to the many hours she spent studying."

ATTRIBUTES — Identifying characteristics, qualities, inherent gifts or talents; generally used in the positive sense. "The *attributes* she brought to her work included a fine mind, superior training and a positive attitude."

B

BENCHMARK — An incident or activity serving as a reference point from the time it occurs. "The day she read her first book served as a *benchmark* against which all her other achievements were measured."

BEVY — A whole lot. A great many. "There were a *bevy* of idioms with which he had to cope."

BLAND — Lacking outstanding features. Generally unremarkable or pale. Not spicy. "When tutoring sessions are too *bland*, we risk losing the student's interest."

BOLSTERING — Encouraging. Shoring up. Supporting. Helping people feel better about themselves. "She was known for her practice of *bolstering* the ego of her students."

BROCHURE — A pamphlet, a booklet, or a flyer telling about a specific activity, cause, or enterprise. "Prepare a *brochure* advertising your tutoring business."

BUGS — Errors in a computer program (software). "She had to work out the *bugs* before the students could use it."

BUREAUCRACY — The organization of an office, especially a government office into bureaus in charge of different tasks. "Prepare questions by writing them down when seeking answers from a *bureaucracy.*"

C

CARDINAL — With reference to numbers these are the "one, two, three, four, etc." counting numbers with which we are most familiar. "She learned to count the *cardinal* numbers forward and backward."

CAUTIONS — Warnings that care is needed. Advanced notices. "There are many practical *cautions* to be observed when working in a carpenter's shop."

CENTIMETER — A metric measurement roughly corresponding to an inch. A hundreth of a meter. "There are one hundred *centimeters* in a meter."

CERTIFICATION — A kind of license. A statement attesting to one's earned eligibility and qualifications. "She needed to obtain state *certification* to teach in an elementary school."

CIRCUMFERENCE — The outer edge of a circle. "There is a universally used formula for finding the measurement of the *circumference* of any given circle."

CLASSIC — Historic. Old fashioned and respected. Also well known. "She gave the *classic* answer to that question, showing that she had read the assignment."

CLASSIFIED — Put into a category or a group with something in common. "He was *classified* as a student who was color blind."

CLIENTS—Those who seek and pay for help from another person. "The tutor reviewed her roster of *clients* weekly."

COMMONALITY—A trait or traits or cause like that or those of someone or something else. "There was an obvious *commonality* of purpose in the bridge group."

COMMUTATIVE—A mathematical property which says an example will result in the same answer whether it is read backward or forward. "Addition and multiplication are *commutative*. (4 + 6 is the same sum as 6 + 4; 8 × 3 is the same total as 3 × 8). Neither subtraction nor division can be *commutative.*"

COMPETENT—Capable of accomplishing tasks and doing them well. Able. "She took pleasure in knowing how *competent* she was as an administrator."

COMPLEX—Intricate. Not simple. Having a variety of mixed qualities. "The three-step math problem proved to be too *complex* for him to handle at this early stage."

COMPREHENSION—The condition of understanding; knowledge. "He showed little *comprehension* of the division process.

CONDUCIVE—Leading to or contributing to a result; well disposed toward; instrumental. "A sunny room is more *conducive* to learning than a drab one."

CONFIGURATIONS—Shapes or formations of patterns. "Gallery paintings were full of geometric *configurations.*"

CONFORM—To be like; to obey; to adjust to what others are doing. "Most teenagers try to *conform* to their peers."

CONJUGATING—Putting verbs into a schematic arrangement—into a format—usually combining them with pronouns. For example, the present tense of the verb to be: I am, you are, he is, she is, we are; you are; they are. "No attention ought to be given to *conjugating* verbs in the early stages of learning a language."

CONSIDERATION—An attitude of concerned feeling for someone or something. "He appreciated the *consideration* the class was showing by waiting for him to catch up."

CONSONANTS—Those letters of the English alphabet which are not vowels: b,c,d,f,g,h,j,k,l,m,n,p,q,r,s,t,v,w,x,z. The letter y is sometimes considered a consonant (play) and sometimes considered a vowel (my, cry, dry). "Although every English word must have a vowel or a 'y'—there are words which have no *consonants.*"

CONSULTANT—A person who is employed or introduced into a situation to provide specific services, generally advisory in nature. "If paid as a *consultant*, a tutor is not on a regular payroll."

CONVERSANT—Familiar with; able to speak about. "The tutor was *conversant* with the problems learning English presents to foreigners."

CONVEYING—Getting across; carrying over to. "His tutor was good at *conveying* the meaning of a selection."

COORDINATION—Meshing. The body's ability to move several of its parts in relative harmony with one another. "Hand-eye *coordination* is a problem for some students."

CORDON—Section off a part of an area from another part. "If you *cordon* off a part of your den to serve as an office, you will let the family know that the space is special."

CREDENTIALS — Papers attesting to the legitimate right of the holder to be doing what he or she is doing. "A college degree and a teacher certification are the *credentials* needed for classroom teaching."

CRITIQUE — An evaluation with comments meant to be helpful, to analyze and to guide. "The tutor's *critique* of her homework showed her what needed improvement."

CRUCIAL — Vital. Extremely important. "It is *crucial* that you be able to read if you hope to get along well in this American environment."

D

DAUNTING — Causing fear or anxiety. "She found the prospect of making a speech so *daunting* that she began to tremble."

DECIPHER — Solve; break a code; translate into understandable form. "It was difficult to *decipher* the message because his handwriting was so poor."

DECLARATIVE — Straightforward. An ordinary sentence that is not a question. "He made his point forcefully with a series of short, *declarative* sentences."

DECODING — Breaking words down into smaller parts to make them more easily readable. "*Decoding* a long word is often the best way to read it."

DEFICIENCY — Lacking in something that is needed in order to perform a task. "He had a coordination *deficiency* that made it difficult for him to read."

DENOMINATOR — The bottom number of a fraction (below the line). "It is almost impossible to add or subtract fractions until you establish a common *denominator.*"

DEVISE — Invent; work out a way to do something. "He was able to *devise* a tool which held the delicate sculpture."

DIAGNOSTIC — Finding what is wrong by examining the symptoms; a test to determine where and what the learning problems are. "Once she had taken the *diagnostic* math test, it became obvious that she could not divide."

DIAMETER — A straight line that passes through the center of a circle dividing it in half. "The *diameter* of a circle is made up of two end-to-end radii."

DICTIONARY — A book in which one can find the spelling, the meaning, the pronunciation and the derivation of words. There are many different kinds of dictionaries devoted to many different purposes. "A picture *dictionary* can be useful in teaching English, even to adults."

DIPHTHONG — Two vowel sounds joined together to make one new sound as in: o i—oil; o u—out. "The students had a special page in their notebooks devoted to *diphthongs.*"

DISCREPANCY — Something which does not match the expected condition or the expected outcome. "Check your bank statements to be sure there is no *discrepancy* in your checkbook balance."

DISPEL — To scatter; to wipe away. "He tried to *dispel* the notion that not being able to read was a mark of low intelligence."

DISTRACTABILITY — Able to have one's attention pulled away from what it ought to be focused on. "An increase in *distractability* can be a sign that a student has lost interest in the lesson."

DISTRIBUTIVE — A mathematical principle which states that if a quantity is distributed to both sides of an equation or an inequality, the result will remain true. (5 + 7 equals 12 would still be true if we add 2 to 5 + 7 and add two to 12. It would become 5 + 7 + 2 equals 12 + 2. "The *distributive* principle is used often in algebra."

DIVIDEND — A number to be divided by another number. "The *dividend* appears inside and the divisor appears outside in a division algorism."

DOCUMENTATION — Supporting papers; proof. "*Documentation* in the form of a birth certificate proved her citizenship."

DOMAIN — A sphere of influence; a territory. "The principal obviously felt that the school was his private *domain.*"

DOMINANCE — Authority or control over. "In the case of mixed-*dominance,* neither the right nor the left side of the brain is consistantly playing the role expected of it."

DUPLICATE — An exact copy. "He has a machine in his office that can produce a *duplicate* of any document."

DUPLICATORS — Machines capable of making exact copies. "There are many different brands of *duplicators* on the market."

DYSLEXIA — A perceptual malfunction that can take different forms. "People who suffer with *dyslexia* have difficulty in reading because they see print in various ways."

E

ECLECTIC — Made up of what seems the best of varied sources. "An *eclectic* approach to teaching reading should be more successful than adherence to any single method."

ELEMENTS — Separate, individual parts which go into making a whole. "Breaking a very long word into its component *elements* may make it more understandable."

ENCODING — Putting parts of a word together to form a whole word (dis taste ful—becomes distasteful). "*Encoding* is a skill we use in both reading and writing."

ENCYCLOPEDIA — A set of reference books containing information on many branches of learning. "An *encyclopedia* will contain short biographies of famous men and women."

ENDEAVORS — Attempts; trying to do something. "He was rewarded for his *endeavors* with a certificate of completion."

ENDORSEMENT — Backing; standing up for; providing documents of approval and recommendation. "She had the *endorsement* of the entire school board when she was hired."

ENGROSSING — Capturing and holding one's attention. "The book about the Civil War was completely *engrossing.*"

ENHANCE — Make something better than it has been. "She learned she could *enhance* tutoring sessions by having her clients take an active part in every lesson."

ENLIGHTENING — Clarifying meaning; uncovering knowledge. "He found the information on the tape *enlightening.*"

ENRICHMENT — Adding to one's knowledge base, especially with other than ordinarily prescribed subject matter. "Once he had mastered the basics, he studied advanced material for the *enrichment* it contributed to his life."

ENTERPRISE — A business organization; an undertaking or a project. "A tutoring business can prove to be a profitable *enterprise.*"

ENTREPRENEUR — A person who establishes, owns, manages and assumes the risks of a business enterprise. "She learned what it meant to be an *entrepeneur* when she launched her learning center."

EQUATIONS — Quantities that are equal to one another. "*Equations* appear in all branches of mathematics."

ESOTERIC — Something not usually understood by the general run of people; different, in a positive, interesting way. "He found the discussion on the meaning of 'good' to be too *esoteric* for him to follow."

ESSENTIAL — Necessary; fundamental. "Knowledge of number facts is *essential* for functioning well in arithmetic."

ESTEEM — Admiration; high regard. "Her self-*esteem* was raised considerably when she could read with ease."

ESTIMATING — Taking a reasonable guess bringing one close to a correct solution. "*Estimating* the result of adding the numbers brought her close to the correct answer."

EXACERBATE — Intensify in a way that makes it worse. "Giving him too hard an assignment will *exacerbate* his problem."

EXCHANGE — The actual process used when we "carry" from one column to another. "Once a student has learned the reason for *exchange,* addition and subtraction become more understandable."

EXPENDITURE — A sum of money spent on paying bills or making some sort of purchase. "Opening a comprehensive learning center will call for an *expenditure* of funds."

F

FACILITY — A building or a part of one used to provide some particular service. "The *facility* which housed the tutoring center had brick sides and stone steps."

FERRET — To dig out; to uncover. "They spent hours trying to *ferret* out the reason for her failure."

FILE — To put away in a classified (generally alphabetical or numerical) order. "She asked him to *file* each student record in its proper alphabetical place."

FISCAL — Relating to financial matters and their time periods. "The *fiscal* year of the learning center began in September."

FLEXIBILITY — Adaptability; amenability; willingness to bend and even acquiesce.

"The tutor showed no *flexibility* when it came to requiring that work be done on time."

FLUENTLY — With ease and control; usually used with relation to handling a language. "Once she lost her anxiety, she was able to speak more *fluently.*"

FORAY — Going in search of; to swoop down upon; to invade. "A *foray* into a new language is hard for most people."

FORMALITIES — Adherence to conventions; the way things are customarily done. "Observing *formalities* is more important in some cultures than in others."

FORMIDABLE — Very challenging and somewhat frightening. "She faced the *formidable* task of learning English."

FORTRAN — A computer language used mostly in the construction of software programs. "*Fortran* is a sophisticated computer language."

FRACTIONAL — Partial. "When we speak of *fractional* parts we refer to measured portions of a whole."

FRANCHISE — A business arrangement (one buys the right to use the name, processes and materials of a parent company and agrees to conform to parent company standards). "Carvel is a *franchise* operation."

FUNCTION — Ability to act in a specific manner. "The *function* of zero in a column of numbers is that of place holder."

FUNCTIONALLY ILLITERATE — Unable to read or write with adequate understanding. "The *functionally illiterate* adult can't enjoy many of the privileges the society offers,"

FUNDAMENTAL — Absolutely basic. "American democracy is based on the *fundamental* truths of equality."

G

GENERALIZE — To transfer what one has learned from individual experiences for use in similar situations. "We are expected to *generalize* once we know a process and use the knowledge for problem solving."

GEOMETRIC — A figure such as a triangle, a circle, a square or a rectangle used in the study of geometry. "The drapes had small *geometric* figures sprinkled over them."

GIST — The general, estimated meaning of something. "Although she did not understand every word, she was able to get the *gist* of the conversation."

GLEANED — Collected a little at a time; skimmed for meaning. "He *gleaned* the approximate meaning of the passage."

GLITCHES — Computer program errors or malfunctions; bugs. "The computer hacker was able to help us eliminate the *glitches* in the program."

GOURMET — Highly specialized taste; very discerning and particular about food. "She specialized in cooking *gourmet* food for the discriminating palate."

GRAPH — A diagram that shows by a system of boxes, lines, or dots the relationships between or among things. "The line graph showed the rise and fall of the market."

GRAPHIC — Very specific; understandable; usually illustrated. "His descriptions of the illness was *graphic* and scary."

GRAPPLING — Struggling with; trying to solve. "He was still *grappling* with the long division problem."

GRATIFYING — Quietly pleasing; rewarding. "It was *gratifying* to realize she was actually able to read at last."

GRID — A format on which one can construct a graph. "The *grid* had small dots in the corner of every square."

H

HARANGUING — Nagging; preaching to in a bothersome manner. "The tutor realized that there was little point in *haranguing* her about her poor handwriting."

HASSLE — A strenuous effort; a struggle. "He thought that the ability to read was worth the *hassle.* "

HIERARCHY — A system of layers or strata; a ranking in terms of importance. "In the *hierarchy* of basic needs, the very first is the need for water."

HONING — Sharpening; attempting to perfect a skill. "Practice in front of a mirror was a way of *honing* her skills."

HORMONAL — Referring to the hormones that cause different reactions in our bodies. "A rush of adrenalin through her body was a *hormonal* reaction."

I

IDIOMATIC — An expression in a language that is peculiar to that language. "The American *idiomatic* expression 'get through' means finish."

ILLITERATE — One who cannot read or write. "Not everyone who is *illiterate* is low in intelligence."

IMAGE — Aspect; a representation of. "The *image* of that rose on the canvas is quite moving."

IMPOSE — To force something on a person. "She tried to *impose* her attitudes on the others in the group."

INADVERTENTLY — Without previous planning; by accident. "She *inadvertently* stumbled on his secret."

INCUMBENT — As used in the text it means something that is a necessary thing for a person to do. "It is *incumbent* upon every student to complete the assigned homework."

INDEX — An alphabetical list of items with page numbers. "Look in the *index* to find the page on fractions."

INEQUALITIES — A statement in which two sides of an "equation" are not equal. "The terms equations and *inequalities* are opposites of one another."

INFINITE — Going on endlessly. "There are an *infinite* number of doubles of any number."

INHERENT — An integral or an essential part of; implied. "*Inherent* in the human spirit is the desire to love."

INNOVATIVE — In a new or imaginative way. "She took an *innovative* way to dealing with the reluctant learner."

INOBTRUSIVELY — Not noticeable or outstanding. "He followed her *inobtrusively.*"

INSPIRATION — A new thought or idea; generally positive. "It was an *inspiration* to challenge them that way."

INTERNALIZE — To make something a part of one's self. "The easiest way to *internalize* a skill is to practice it."

INTERSECT — To cross over. "At the point at which those two lines *intersect* you will find the answer."

INTERSPERSE — To scatter through what is already there. "When you *intersperse* red threads with white your cloth will seem to be pink."

INTONATION — A way of using one's voice or accenting language when speaking. "Northern and southern *intonation* are quite different in American speech."

INTRICACY — Complex and complicated. "The *intricacy* of the situation defied any quick solutions."

INVALUABLE — Worth more than any value ascribed to it. "The ability to read is invaluable."

INVERSIONS — Turning things upside down. "Using *inversions* is generally necessary in dividing fractions."

INVESTMENT — Putting something of one's self or one's money into a project. "*Investment* of effort is necessary in learning something new."

IRRELEVANT — Not related to the matter at hand. "A student's poor past performance ought to be *irrelevant* to tutors."

K

KEYBOARD — The typewriter-like portion of a computer. "The *keyboard* is what is used to interact with a computer."

KILOGRAMS — A metric unit of weight of one thousand grams. "Europeans express weight in *kilograms,* not pounds."

L

LABYRINTH — A winding maze difficult to escape from. "He was caught in a *labyrinth* of lies since he couldn't read."

LAUNCH — Set out; begin; start up. "Beginning to tutor for pay is a way to *launch* yourself into the business world."

LEGIBLY — Written so that it can be read. "Too many people are unable to write a sentence *legibly.*"

LETHARGIC — Sluggish; dull; lazy; apathetic. "She found that students became *lethargic* halfway through each session."

LIABILITY — Having legal responsibility for; opposite of an asset. "A loan will be a *liability* for a while."

LINGUAL — Referring to languages. "Bi-*lingual* means speaking two languages; multi-*lingual* — speaking many languages."

LITER – A measure of volume. "In the metric system a *liter* is roughly equivalent to a quart."

LOGOED – Having an identifying symbol (a logo) applied to something. "Her business card is *logoed* with a pencil."

M

MANIPULATIVE – Used with word "material" to mean a learning aid that can be felt, handled and moved about. "Using *manipulative* materials help children to learn more easily."

MAXIMUM – The largest possible amount. "The *maximum* amount of liquid that container will hold is one pint."

MENTOR – An active sponsor. "Volunteering to serve as a *mentor* to a young person is giving that person a special gift."

METHODOLOGY – Techniques one uses in presenting knowledge and information to others. "The *methodology* a tutor chooses will determine the rate of success of his students."

METRIC – A system of weights and measures used in most of the countries of the world. "It is a problem for older folks to transfer thinking from standard measures to metric."

MILIEU – Environment, including the ambience or atmosphere. "The *milieu* in which that child lives is threatening."

MILLIMETER – A metric measure about four tenths of an inch. "We can express length of small things in *millimeters.*"

MINIMAL – Very little; about as small as possible. "You ought to have a *minimal* amount of disturbance when you tutor."

MITIGATING – Modifying or making less difficult. "*Mitigating* circumstances let him graduate with his class."

MNEMONIC – A memory device usually made up by the learners to help them remember something lengthy or complicated. "My Very Excited Mother Just Stood Up Near Pop—is a handy *mnemonic* for remembering the planets in their relation to the sun. (Mercury, Venus, Earth, Mars, Jupiter, Saturn, Uranus, Neptune, Pluto.)"

MODEM – A device which attaches to a computer and a telephone line and accesses data banks. "His *modem* gave him access to 'bulletin boards' throughout the country."

MODIFICATIONS – Changes; either increases or decreases. "She made several *modifications* in her programs."

MONITOR – The screen portion of a computer. "The *monitor* of my computer cannot provide me with color."

MORES – Cultural ways or customs of a group. "Understanding the *mores* of your students keeps you from offending."

MORPHEME – A meaningful linguistic unit that contains no smaller parts (at, and, or). "Starting with a *morpheme,* we can affix letters and syllables to build words."

MOTIVATORS – Things that make people want to learn or do. "Good *motivators* stimulate students to work hard."

MOUSE – An attachment to a computer which can gain one access to programs without using the keyboard. "If a *mouse* comes with your computer, you can sketch with it."

MUNDANE – Ordinary; not unusual. "The most *mundane* tasks can often be made to seem exciting by a good tutor."

MYRIAD – A very great many. "The *myriad* of new words she was expected to learn in a short time seemed overwhelming."

N

NEGATIVE NUMBER – A quantity less than zero. "Two *negative* numbers added together result in a larger negative."

NEGOTIATING – Conferring, with the goal of arriving at a settlement of a matter in contention. "The union was negotiating with the school board for a new contract."

NOUNS – Grammatical term for words which name persons, places or things. "A *noun* can be the subject of a sentence."

NUMBER – The actual quantity referred to when we use numerals as their representatives. "The quantity ten is a *number* while the symbol '10' is a numeral."

NUMERALS – The written symbols we use to indicate the amounts we are working with. "We use both Arabic (1, 2, 3, 4, 5, etc.) and Roman (I, II, V, IX, etc.) *numerals* to represent numbers or quantities."

O

OBLIGATE – To bind one to perform in some way. "He refused to *obligate* himself to be a volunteer."

ONE – Used here as the identity element for multiplication and division. "Any number multiplied or divided by one will not change its value."

OPTHALMOLOGIST – A physician who specializes in diagnosis and treatment of diseases and malfunctions of the eyes. "Any person with dyslexia should see an *ophthalmologist.*"

OPTIONS – A set of choices. "He had many *options* when it came to deciding what he wanted to tutor."

ORDINAL – A way of expressing placement of numbers relative to one another. "The *ordinal* numbers are: first, second, third, fourth, fifth, etc."

ORDINANCES – Legal regulations passed by local governments. "The city council passed several *ordinances* related to trash disposal."

ORIENTATION – An introduction to a new condition or group; a positioning with reference to place. "She was asked to attend an *orientation* session for new teachers."

ORIGINALS – Uncopied and therefore (generally) unique. "All of the paintings were *originals* created by her students."

OVERHEAD — The basic, repetitive costs of running a business operation. "Rent, heat, electricity, water, and phone services are *overhead* business expenses."

OVERWHELM — To submerge completely; to subdue. "It is not a good idea to *overwhelm* students with homework."

P

PARTICIPATE — Take part in; join in with. "She was too shy to *participate* in most classroom activities."

PATRONIZED — Treated as an inferior. "She felt *patronized* because of the way he ignored everything she said."

PC'S — PERSONAL COMPUTERS. "There are so many *PC's* on the market, it is difficult to know what to buy."

PERCEPTUAL — Relating to how one sees and how one interprets what one sees. "A *perceptual* disorder can interfere with the ability to learn how to read and write."

PERIMETER — The outer edge of a geometric figure. "There was a fence around the *perimeter* of the entire property."

PERIODIC — At stated times. "The supervisor came to visit the class at *periodic* intervals."

PERIODICALS — A publication published at stated intervals. "He had bookshelves in his office filled with *periodicals.*"

PERPENDICULAR — At right angles to something. "The building's sides stood exactly *perpendicular* to the sidewalk."

PERSEVERATION — Inability to shift easily from one word to another or from one meaning to another when reading. "She was able to diagnose the student's problem as a case of *perseveration.*"

PERTAINING — With reference to. "He claimed that he had to do something *pertaining* to his job, so he could not come."

PHONEME — One of the smallest units of speech distinguishing one sound from another. "We get the word phonics from the word *phoneme.*"

PHONETICS — A system of classification of the sounds in a language. "Using symbols of *phonetics,* we can write a correct pronunciation of a word."

PORTFOLIO — An envelope-like container for carrying papers or other materials. "It is important for a tutor to create a *portfolio* describing his credentials."

POTENT — Powerful; virile; full of potential. "Reading is a *potent* asset to learning."

POTENTIAL — Something that has the possibility of expanding or changing. "An intelligent person should do everything she can to develop her *potential* as a scholar."

PREFIX — An affix occurring at the beginning of a word. "The *prefix* 're' before a verb usually means to do again."

PRIORITY — A consideration which rates a very high degree of importance. "For a good salesman, closing a sale is a high *priority* matter."

PROACTIVE — Taking an action before it becomes necessary; opposite of reactive. "If you plan well you will be able to take *proactive* rather than reactive steps to help."

PROFICIENT — Skillful; able; well practiced. "The way he works on problems shows that he is *proficient* in math."

PROFOUNDLY — Very deeply; very seriously. "She was *profoundly* moved by the story of her escape from Viet Nam."

PROMINENT — Standing out; easily noticeable; well known. "Many *prominent* people came to the opening."

PROSPECTIVE — Something about to happen. "She was looking forward to the *prospective* opening of the center."

PROVINCE — The proper scope of; an area of influence. "Fixing what is wrong is the *province* of the tutor."

PRUDENT — Carefully wise. "If you are *prudent* in the way you spend money, you may be able to save some."

Q

QUARTERS — The result when one has cut something into four pieces; also refers to places to stay. "She had the pie cut into *quarters* so that each of the four bridge players could have a portion."

QUIXOTIC — Easily changeable; impractical. "His *quixotic* behavior was unpredictable."

R

RADIUS — A line from the center of a circle to its perimeter. "A *radius* is half the length of a diameter."

RAM — A computer term meaning random access memory. "The *RAM* of that PC is large enough to meet his writing needs."

RATIO — The relationship between quantities. "The *ratio* of income to outgo is positive."

RECEPTORS — Sensory organs on a biological individual or on a machine or electronic device. "As long as the animal's *receptors* are functioning it will react."

REGULATIONS — Rules defining how laws are to be carried out. "There are *regulations* to follow when in business."

REINFORCEMENT — Strengthening; practice, to fix learning. "She gave her a number of examples for *reinforcement.*"

RELUCTANT — Not willing; somewhat resistant. "The tall man was *reluctant* to admit that he could not read the menu."

REMEDIATION — Assistance to help correct a negative condition. "The reading clinic was set up to provide *remediation.*"

RENDITION — A performance, usually of something artistic. "The music student's *rendition* of the concerto was masterful."

RESOURCE — A person, place, or thing to go to for assistance or for information. "The public library in every town is an excellent *resource* for locating information."

RESUME — A document presenting information and credentials of a person; a "vita." "Her *resume* indicated that she had spent many years as a classroom teacher."

REVERSALS — Turnarounds. "Seeing *saw* when the written word is *was* is an example of a *reversal.*"

ROSTER — A list, generally of people's names. "She was on the *roster* of people to be called in case of an emergency."

ROTE — Memorizing; being able to repeat by heart. "He could recite it by *rote* but didn't know what it meant."

RUDIMENTS — Elementary principles or basics. "He had grasped the *rudiments* of math but stopped there."

S

SCANNING — Passing the eye quickly over something and getting an overall message rather than a word-for-word message. "He relied on his *scanning* ability to learn the nature of the magazine."

SCOFF — Downplay; jeer at; refuse to take seriously. "She had to *scoff* at his claim to be an expert."

SENSORY — Relating to the use of the five senses. "She based her tutoring on sensory stimulation."

SESSIONS — Blocks of time devoted to a set of tasks such as tutoring, for example. "She contracted for a dozen *sessions* with the tutor."

SIGNIFICANT — Something that matters very much; something of importance. "There was *significant* improvement apparent after only a few months."

SIMMER DOWN — An idiomatic expression meaning to get a hold on one's temper. "He was quick to *simmer down* after his unexpected outburst."

SOCIALIZING — Used to mean helping children learn what the society expects of them. "Parents play a primary role in *socializing* their children."

SOFTWARE — Programs used by computers to perform functions. "The *software* we bought for writing is Wordstar."

SPARSE — Very few available; widely distributed. "The learning materials were *sparse* in that classroom."

SPECTRUM — A continuous sequence or a wide range. "The whole *spectrum* of colors exist in a rainbow."

SPREAD SHEET — A helpful format for keeping track of business income and expenditures. "The spread sheet format gives a business person an overview of her finances."

STANDARDIZED — Usually referring to tests that have been made uniform so results can be compared. "The SAT is an example of a widely used *standardized* test.

STRATEGIES — Plans or methods for achieving desirable ends. "Use a variety of *strategies* to help people learn."

SUBDIVISIONS — Parts of a whole. "The American government has a multitude of subdivisions."

SUBSTANTIAL — Sturdy; reliable. "He had *substantial* background in the area of automotive work."

SUFFIX — An affix used at the end of a word. "One of the most used *suffixes* in English is 'ing'."

SURGE SUPPRESSOR — A device used to keep electric current from surging into an electronic mechanism. "My computer is plugged into a *surge suppressor.*"

SYMBOLS — Letters, numbers, or pictures used to stand for something else. "*Symbols* on restroom doors tell even the illiterate which is for men and which is for women."

SYMMETRY — Evenness. "*Symmetry* is one of the principles all artists can choose to use or ignore."

T

TABULA RASA — A blank tablet; coming new to something with no previous knowledge or experience. "Many believe that all babies come into the world as *tabula rasa.*"

TANGIBLE — Touchable. Something you can feel and, by extension, understand and believe in. "All of the lessons in her sessions rely on *tangible* materials."

TERMINAL — One of the devices that is part of a computer used either for input or output. "A printer is a *terminal* for a computer."

TESTS — Instruments used to evaluate performance. "There are *tests* available for diagnosing learning difficulties."

TEXT — A book organized in an orderly way to present material to be learned. "A math *text* is a helpful resource."

TEXTUAL — Referring to material in a textbook. "Any lesson dependent only on *textual* material is bound to be dull."

THEOREMS — Mathematical statements to be proven. "He asked her to prove the *theorem* of equal angles of a square."

THESAURUS — A reference dictionary of synonyms. "Roget is the author of the best-known *thesauraus.*"

TREASURE TROVE — A very valuable discovery. "Modems have given us access to a *treasure trove* of information."

TUTOR — A person who helps others to learn. "If you wish to be a paid *tutor,* this book will be very helpful to you."

U

UNFATHOMABLE — Almost impossible to understand. "Tutors help people work through what had seemed *unfathomable.*"

UNIQUE — One of a kind; different; special. "She was proud of her *unique* talent."

UNVARYING — Completely dependable; unchanging. "His loyalty was *unvarying.*"

V

VARIANCE — A legal term meaning an exception to a regulation. "He applied for a *variance* and was granted permission to work from his home."

VERBATIM — Exactly, word-for-word. "She repeated the story *verbatim.*"

VISUAL — Something appearing to the eye; a picture, slide, movie, etc. "The *visual* appeal of his surroundings made one want to study with him."

VITA — A resume. "She handed the prospective employer a copy of her *vita* and left."

VITAL — Necessary. "It was *vital* that she be able to meet the payroll at the end of every month."

VITALIZE — To inspire, reinvigorate, and breathe energy into. "He did his best to *vitalize* his tutoring sessions."

VOWEL — Those letters of the alphabet that are sounded. "There are five *vowels*, a, e, i, o, u; the letter y is sometimes considered a vowel."

W

WORD PROCESSING — A computer program that allows words to be entered and produces printed pages. "A *word processing* program makes writing easier than using a typewriter."

Y

YIELD — Produce; give off. "The farm *yield* last year was lower than for several previous years."

Z

ZERO — The identity element for addition and subtraction. "Adding a zero to, or subtracting a zero from, any number will result in no change in the number."

ZONING — Regulations restricting the kinds of activities which may be conducted in certain areas of towns or cities. "If the *zoning* in the area where you live is restrictive, you may not be able to conduct tutoring sessions at home."

BIBLIOGRAPHY

Azar, Betty Schrampfer. *Understanding and Using English Grammar.* Englewood Cliffs, New Jersey: Prentice-Hall Regents, 1989.

Baughman, Dale M. *Educator's Handbook of Stories, Quotes And Humor.* Englewood Cliffs, New Jersey: Prentice-Hall, Inc., 1963.

Buros, O.K. *Mental Measurements Yearbook, Ninth Edition.* Edited by James Mitchell. Highland Park, New Jersey: 1985.

Chamot, Anna U., and O'Malley, Michael J. *Language Development Through Content— Mathematics Book A.* Learning Strategies For Problem Solving. Reading, Massachusettes: Addison-Wesley, 1988.

De Angeli, Marguerite. *Book of Nursery and Mother Goose Rhymes.* New York: Doubleday & Company, Inc., 1954.

Fry, Edward B., Polk, Jacqueline K., and Fountoukidis, Dona. *The Reading Teacher's Book of Lists.* Englewood Cliffs, New Jersey: Prentice-Hall, Inc., 1984.

Gorn, Janice L. *The Writer's Handbook.* New York: Monarch Press, 1984.

Hall, Nancy A. *Rescue.* A Handbook of Remedial Reading Techniques. Stevensville, Michigan: Educational Service, Inc., 1969.

Hanson, Marie, and Bessey, Barbra. *Tutor Training Guide—English As A Second Language.* A Set Of Five Modules For Use In Training Volunteer ESL Tutors. Portland, Oregon: Chemeketa Community College Press, 1988.

Mitchell, Steve. *How To Speak Southern.* Illustrated by Scrawls. New York: Bantam Books, 1980.

Moran, Patrick R. *Lexicary. An Illustrated Vocabulary Builder for Second Languages.* Supplementary Materials Handbook #2. Brattleboro, Vermont: Pro Lingua Associates, 1984.

Platts, Mary E. *Spice.* Stevensville, Michigan: Educational Service Inc., 1970.

Rodale, J.J. *The Synonym Finder.* Emmaus, Pennsylvania: Rodale Press, 1978.

Sisson, A.F. *Sisson's Word And Expression Locator.* West Nyack, New York: Parker Publishing Co., 1966.

Trager, Edith Crowell. *PD's In Depth Pronunciation—Aural Discrimination Drills for Learners of English.* Englewood Cliffs, New Jersey: Prentice-Hall, Inc., 1982.

Warriner, John E., and Griffith, Francis. *Warriner's English Grammar and Composition.* Complete Course. New York: Harcourt Brace Jovanovich, 1977.

INDEX